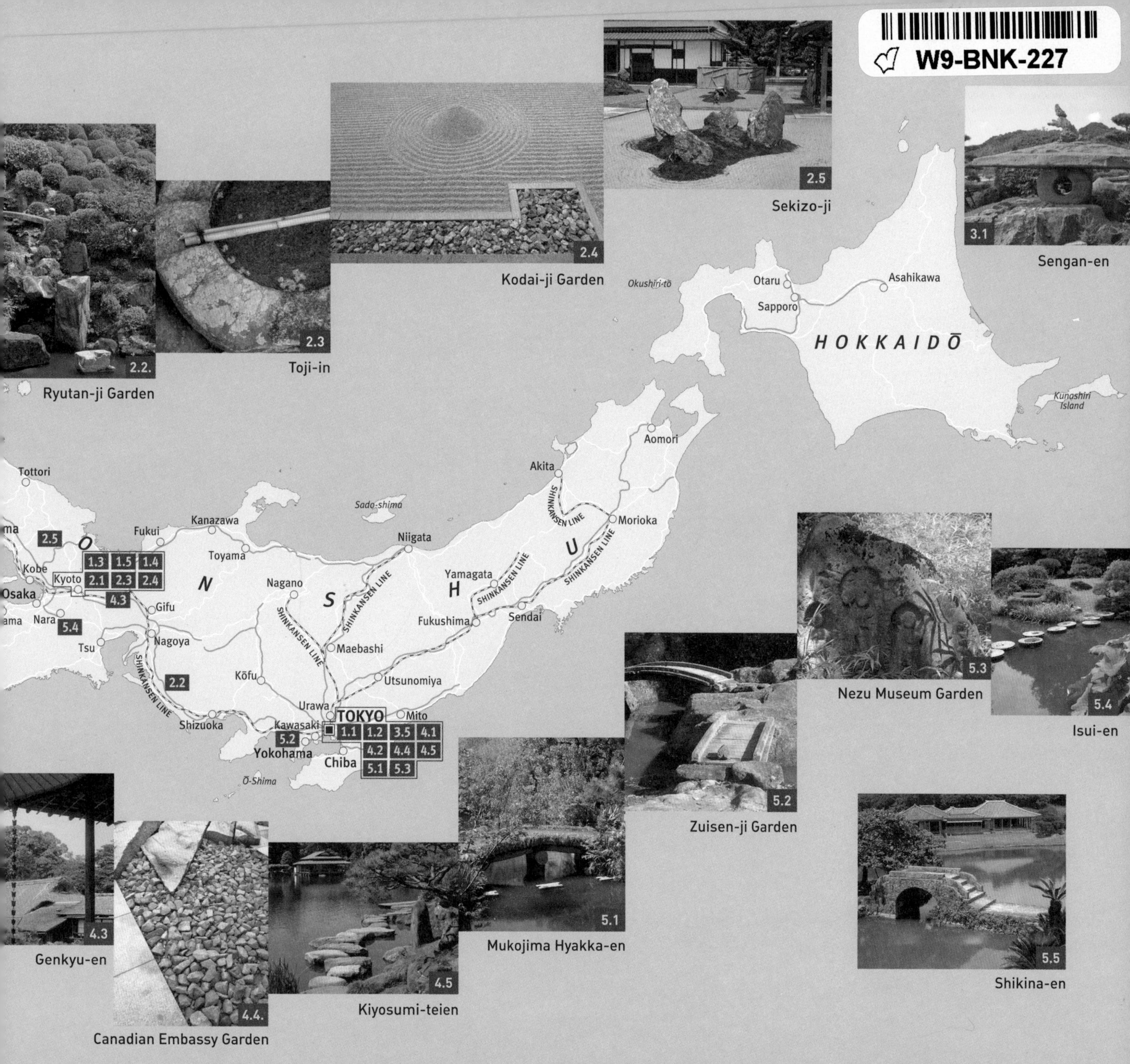
W9-BNK-227
2.5
Sekizo-ji
2.4
Kodai-ji Garden
3.1
Sengan-en
2.3
Toji-in
2.2.
Ryutan-ji Garden
Okushiri-tō
Otaru
Sapporo
Asahikawa
HOKKAIDŌ
Kunashiri Island
Aomori
Akita
Tottori
Sado-shima
Kanazawa
Fukui
Niigata
Toyama
Morioka
Yamagata
Sendai
Fukushima
Nagano
Maebashi
Utsunomiya
Kyoto
Kobe
Osaka
Nara
Gifu
Nagoya
Tsu
Kōfu
Shizuoka
Urawa
TOKYO
Mito
Kawasaki
Yokohama
Chiba
Ō-Shima
SHINKANSEN LINE
O N S H U
2.5
1.3 1.5 1.4
2.1 2.3 2.4
4.3
5.4
2.2
5.2
1.1 1.2 3.5 4.1
4.2 4.4 4.5
5.1 5.3
5.3
Nezu Museum Garden
5.4
Isui-en
5.2
Zuisen-ji Garden
5.1
Mukojima Hyakka-en
5.5
Shikina-en
4.3
Genkyu-en
4.4.
Canadian Embassy Garden
4.5
Kiyosumi-teien

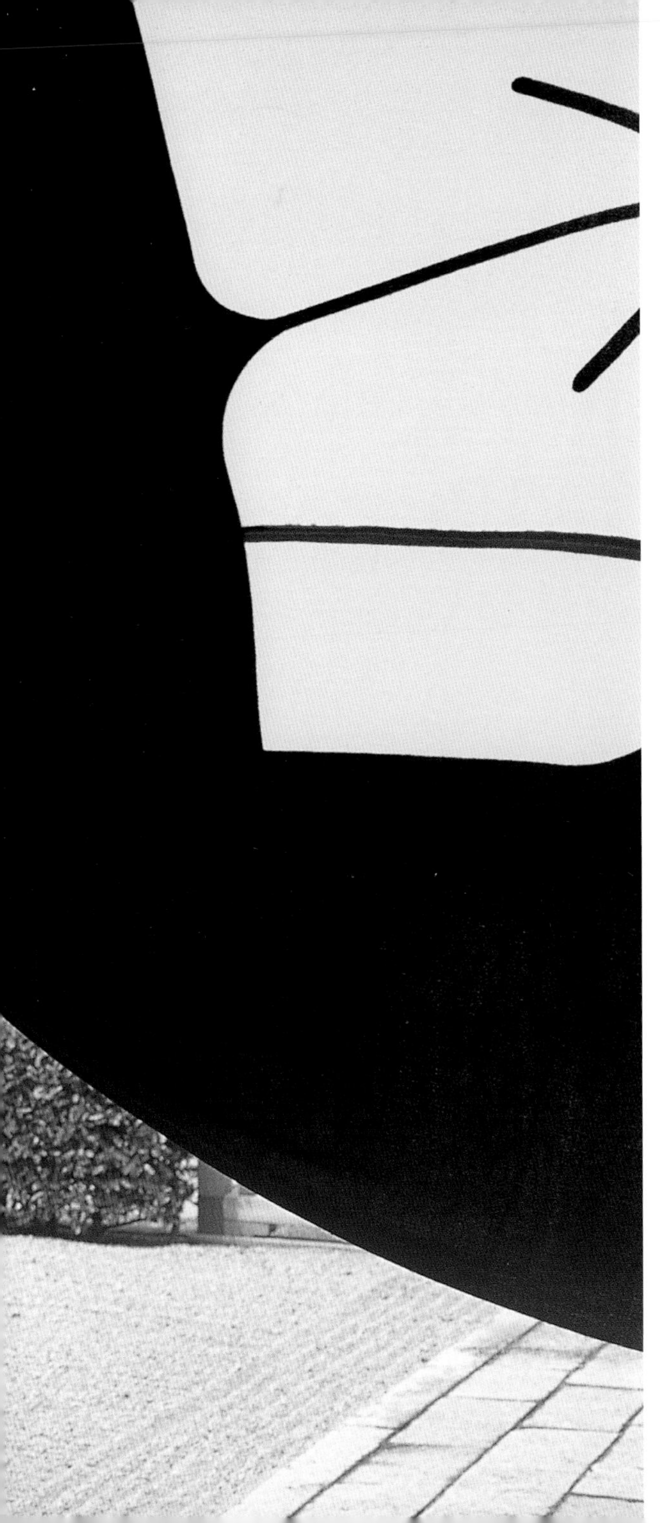

Japan's Master Gardens

Lessons in Space and Environment

Stephen Mansfield

TUTTLE Publishing

Tokyo | Rutland, Vermont | Singapore

Published by Tuttle Publishing, an imprint of Periplus Editions (HK) Ltd

www.tuttlepublishing.com

Library of Congress Cataloging-in-Publication Data

Mansfield, Stephen.
Japan's master gardens : lessons in space and environment / Stephen Mansfield.
p. cm.
Includes bibliographical references.
ISBN 978-4-8053-1128-8 (hardcover)
1. Gardens, Japanese--History. 2. Gardens--Japan--Design--History. I. Title.
SB458.M36 2012
712.0952--dc23
2011019342

ISBN: 978-4-8053-1128-8

Distributed by

North America, Latin America & Europe
Tuttle Publishing, 364 Innovation Drive
North Clarendon, VT 05759-9436 USA
Tel: 1 (802) 773-8930; Fax: 1 (802) 773-6993
info@tuttlepublishing.com; www.tuttlepublishing.com

Japan
Tuttle Publishing, Yaekari Building, 3rd Floor
5-4-12 Osaki, Shinagawa-ku, Tokyo 141-0032
Tel: (81) 3 5437-0171, Fax: (81) 3 5437-0755
sales@tuttle.co.jp, www.tuttle.co.jp

Asia Pacific
Berkeley Books Pte. Ltd.
61 Tai Seng Avenue, #02-12, Singapore 534167
Tel: (65) 6280-1330, Fax: (65) 6280-6290
inquiries@periplus.com.sg; www.periplus.com

15 14 13 12 1111EP
5 4 3 2 1

Printed in Hong Kong

contents

Preface

Garden nature, like human nature, requires care and nurturing if it is not to lead to a kind of inanition.

Pondering the fate of the Japanese garden, the Meiji era writer Lafcadio Hearn wrote: "These are the gardens of the past. The future will know them only as dreams, creations of a forgotten art." In this respect, thankfully, he was wrong.

How is it possible, though, to enjoy peace and tranquility, to savor Japanese gardens as healing, regenerative spaces when they have become so popular? Victims of their own success, whatever mystic or higher qualities they once had are at risk of being drowned out by the din of over-patronage. Japanese master gardens, however, may still offer alternative models for environmental enhancement. The purifying sensation one experiences on entering a garden affirms its power to promote a healthy emotional and spiritual life. In mirroring our yearning for stability and peace, our search for a settled place, its paths return us to our original nature.

In exploring the garden, we are making renewed contact with Japanese culture. Once we have understood one form, we may more readily appreciate another. In appropriating differing elements of Japanese culture, the Japanese garden prepares us for an examination of other arts and practices. Japanese aesthetics, the fine-tuning of taste, the development of connoisseurship through the appreciation of beauty, came later than the proto-gardens of the pre-Shinto era, but the transition from divine nature to art was relatively seamless. And yet, the revisualization of nature that takes place through the filtration of art in the Japanese garden is often quite different from what we are accustomed to. Disarmed, for example, by the vision of compositions purporting to be landscape works but made entirely of stone and gravel, we are forced to reconsider the place of nature in the garden, where appearances can be deceptive. The painter David Hockney, whose photomontages of the Ryoan-ji garden in Kyoto are playful reinterpretations of time and space, recognized this when he wrote: "Surface is an illusion, but so is depth."

As a photographer, I am forced to view and analyze the Japanese garden through a lens. While shying away from discussing the variations in approach between Japanese and Western photographers, there do appear to be differences in the way their garden books are illustrated. It may be a case of suggestion and inference versus definition. When the light in a garden is flat, the Western photographer is apt to reject the image as dull, even lachrymose. Japanese photographers, on the other hand, who are masters of the tripod and long exposure, will exult in the muted tones. In this book, I have tried to steer a middle course, one that nonetheless instinctively embraces light that can turn gardens into scenes as radiant as stained glass.

In photographing these gardens, I opted to work with only 50 mm and 24 mm lenses, ones that closely

Opposite A finely leveled water laver provides a horizontal plane from which to appreciate the contours of Chishaku-in temple garden.

conform to what the eye sees, and to use a very slow slide film, one that captures rather better the warmth and texture of gardens than the super-heated, manipulated colors of digital imagery.

So rich in detail are even the simplest of gardens that although we may never entirely comprehend their full meaning, we never tire of them; they can be visited time and again, always revealing something new. Preconceived, concisely framed, the Japanese garden may be an artifact but it reflects the dual characteristics of nature: vitality and serenity. In an age of hyper-materialism and excess, gardens offer an alternative vision. Restricted in space but boundless, transfixed in time yet temporal, the garden sanctuary, its changes as slow as those of a sundial, enables an unhurried contemplation of the beauty of the earth. In creating a state in which time is decelerated, gardens soothe our restlessness, freeing the mind from its habit of perpetual motion.

Sanctuaries have always been places where people retreat to find themselves, approach nature, their own gods. Here, we recognize that the garden's balanced, harmonious environs are similar to what we seek in our own lives. A point of departure, a confrontation with memory or the self, the garden is not a final destination. It occupies a transitional, intermediate space through which we pass, emerging rejuvenated, better able to cope. Gardens may not change our life, but they can improve it immeasurably.

Stephen Mansfield

CHAPTER 1

a sense of nature

WHEN THE ENGLISH POET James Kirkup wrote of the "neat, tremendous garden of Japan," he was referring to both the lushness and the orderliness of nature. That gardens in Japan can be almost voluptuous in their richness yet display deliberate organization and intent, illustrates an intriguing composite of wilderness and methodical design.

It is not surprising that in a country where nature has long been permeated with the spiritual, its most iconic symbol is neither a building nor a monument but a sacred mountain—Fuji-san. Japan's physical forms have exerted a powerful influence on garden design. Its riverbeds, mountains and waterfalls are replicated in almost every garden.

If *kami* (gods) and other natural forces were inherent in nature, they were also present in the earliest known landscape designs. Garden authority Marc P. Keane has written of the *Nihon Shoki*, a chronicle of ancient Japan, that the work alludes to a time when "the trees and grasses had the power of speech." The phrase refers to the perception of nature as an animate, articulate force. Natural objects that emitted a spiritual aura (a rock, a tree, a waterfall) were deified, marked as vectors for the gods, passages through which they could connect with man. Elected natural phenomena, symbolizing the interconnectedness of man and nature, were called *go-shintai*, "dwellings of the gods." Making an enclosure, establishing boundaries, marks the beginning of an ordered space. When the first gardens were eventually made, they were not created to oppose nature but to complement it.

Opposite The effect of moss growing on ancient stone, in this case a water basin, is highly prized by the Japanese.

Above A concentrated, highly controlled design placed beside a naturalistic setting creates both tonal and spatial depth.

Opposite Chinese scholars and poets found nature and the representation of natural forms in garden settings congenial to their lifestyles. The script is in Chinese.

The word *niwa* (garden) first appears in the *Nihon Shoki*, where it refers to a spot that has been purified for the worship of the gods. The central feature of these sanctified spaces was a massive stone called the *iwakura* or *iwasaka*. Where these stones still exist, their sacred character is indicated by ritual rice-fiber ropes called *shimenawa*, and talismanic folded white paper chains known as *gohei*.

The practice of supplicating the sun goddess at the start of the rice season, at enclosures temporarily set up on riverbanks, may have transformed into the area of pebble or gravel found at many Shinto shrines. The desire to view natural landscapes in sanctified settings was evident in the choice of beautiful wooded areas for the placement of shrines.

Requisitioning Nature

The three traditions of Shintoism, Taoism and Buddhism embody a desire for harmony and balance within a vast complex of ideas in which spirit and matter are understood to be in a state of permanent flux. To the Japanese mind, these orthodoxies represented the model of an ordered universe. Although few people possessed a thorough understanding of the collective insight and wisdom of these traditions, the notion that Taoism, with its doctrine of surrender to positive non-action, offered harmony in the body and elemental world, Shinto harmony with the natural world, and Buddhism mental composure, was intuitively understood and accepted. The Taoist idea of the harmony of opposites, of oneness with the fluctuations of nature applicable to garden principles, is apparent in this ancient Chinese verse:

An omen of the winds of decline exists
in the center of plenitude.
The mechanisms of germination exist
in the midst of ruin.

The Jin Dynasty Chinese painter Zong Bing (375–443), drawn to the craggy peaks and precipices of his native landscapes, commented: "They have a material existence and yet reach into a spiritual domain," one possessing a "joy which is of the soul." A sense of this spirit-inhabited world, an *anima mundi*, was echoed in the thoughts of the Zen master Sojo (384–414) when he wrote:

Heaven and earth and I are of the same root,
The ten-thousand things and I are of one substance.

The ancient Chinese world, to which early Japanese civilization was hugely beholden, made no distinction between animate and inanimate. In its estimation, natural phenomena and human life were infused with the psychophysical presence of *qi*, an energy whose polarities were *yin* and *yang*.

A sensitivity to nature meant an awareness of the forces flowing through it. This intuition of powerful currents surging through the earth and air was given authority with the practice of Chinese *feng shui*. In garden terms, interpreting these forces rather than opposing them required the skillful placement of buildings and landscape elements into positions that would accommodate those currents and promote stability. Easily misconstrued with the mystical or superstitious, *feng shui* is grounded in sound environmental practices that take advantage of natural energy flows determined by the contours of landscape. Knowledge of these natural forces was a prerequisite to making a garden.

The *Sakuteiki*, an esoteric eleventh-century garden manual not intended for circulation among the general public, was compiled by the poet and courtier Tachibana no Toshitsuna. The text contains fundamental principles of geomancy. To promote positive outcomes, for example, it advocates, “water must flow in from the east, pass beneath the floor of the house and flow out to the southwest. For in this

Above The trilogy of stone, water and lotuses is suggestive of a sacred garden site.

manner the waters of the Blue Dragon will wash away all the evil spirits from the house and garden and carry them to the White Tiger."

Garden writer Itoh Teiji contended that Japanese garden designers deliberately misinterpreted imported concepts, permitting "distorted versions of foreign ideas to exist side by side with primitive, indigenous garden forms." The *Sakuteiki* is an early indicator of this pliability of approach. The manual advocates that seven maples can substitute for the highway to the west, that three cypress trees suffice for the mountains to the north, that the eastern river can be substituted by nine willows, and that the southern pond might be served symbolically by nine Judas trees. Here we see the Japanese gardener placing expediency and aesthetic preference over literal interpretation.

Gardens of Earth and Heaven

Formal gardens have existed in Japan since the sixth century. Early landscape designs were closely based on ancient Chinese and Korean models, but under the growing influence of Buddhism began to mirror images of Amida's Western Paradise. In order to create a harmonious environment, to unify temples and residences with gardens, the Japanese sought to introduce the exterior into the interior, the inside to the outer world through a series of architectural devices such as sliding doors and movable walls and panels. When a portion of a wall was removed, the room was able to flow into the garden. By extending the flooring of a room to the outside, the wood became an outer verandah or deck space cantilevered above the garden.

The Heian period (794–1185) garden had already begun to incorporate optical effects that projected foreground into the distance and, under the sway of Buddhist teachings on the ceaseless cycles of birth, death and rebirth, turned the seasons into dioramas of eternity. In this representational world, rock groupings, plant arrangements and islands were understood as references to Chinese and Japanese literature. An outcrop of stones and pine trees might evoke Ama-no-hashidate in the west of Japan, or the islands of Matsushima to the northeast; a tortoise-shaped island would represent longevity, other island groupings the mythical isles of the Chinese Immortals. Symbolism and design had come to be used not only to add depth to the garden but, through an unfolding of associations, to expand the spatial aspects of the mind.

Applying the principles of Japanese garden design, its restrictions, observances and freedoms, the gardener converts nature into expressive forms. When it refers to "designing with the mood of harmony," the *Sakuteiki* urges gardeners to draw out and evoke the spirit of nature, not to imitate it. Because nature is inimitable, we cannot replicate it but we may absorb its wisdom.

> *Learn of the pine from the pine: learn of the bamboo from the bamboo.* —Matsuo Basho

Japanese gardens may contain natural features but the principles of gardening imply a collaboration between the natural and the contrived. As Donald Richie has written: "Nature does not happen; it is wrought. A new rule offers itself: nothing is natural until it has been so created." Japanese gardens are the creation of nature only to the extent that nature has a hand in dictating their design and form. Nature being universal, Japanese gardens are a transcultural art.

There are distinct differences, however, in conception and implementation. Traditional garden designers try to make contact with the spirit of the site before they construct the garden, to assist in expressing the garden's *fusui*, its spirit of place, the poetic character and emotion indicative of its intrinsic scenic nature. Designing dry landscapes is as much about hearing as seeing. Traditional garden designers often talk about "listening" to the rocks before they proceed to build a landscape. Zen writer Alan Watts contended that the designer of stone gardens "has no mind to impose his own intention upon natural forms, but is careful rather to follow the 'intentionless intention' of the forms themselves." This is not as unfathomable as it sounds, being consistent with the admonitions contained in the *Sakuteiki*, in which the term *kohan ni shitagau*, "following the request," is used. In practice, the manual advocates listening to the "request" of rocks found on the design site before proceeding to create a waterfall, stream, pond or island. Shunmyo Masuno, a Zen priest and prominent contemporary garden designer, echoes the idea when he contends that when arranging rocks one must "converse" with the stone, waiting "until it seems to speak and say where it wants to be put."

Japanese gardening, then, is a collaboration between man and nature, moderated by the slow passage of time. Mature gardens contain the material outlines, the trapped sensations and essences of an older Japan. It is possible in the rock patterns, gnarled trees, winding stone paths, lotus ponds, and in the sinuous lines raked in sand and gravel to discover principles consonant with older beliefs and traditions, an almost hieratic order present beneath the moldering stone and hoary bark.

Shinjuku Gyoen

新宿御園

Type **Composite parkland, Japanese, Western gardens**
Period **Early 20th century**
Location **Naitocho, Shinjuku-ku, Tokyo**

Left The Japanese section of the park, seen from inside the Taiwan Pavilion, built in 1928 to commemorate the wedding of the Emperor Hirohito.
Right Late October to November sees the erection of several beautifully crafted chrysanthemum pavilions in which imaginative displays are exhibited.

Sitting at the head of the Shibuya River system, the well-watered gardens at Shinjuku Gyoen were completed in 1772, after the *shogun* bequeathed the estate to Lord Naito, the *daimyo* of Tsuruga. Following the Meiji Restoration of 1869, the manor and its grounds were converted into an agricultural experimentation center and then into a botanical garden. The grounds became an imperial property in 1879. The current landscaping was completed in 1906.

Much of the garden at Shinjuku Gyoen was destroyed in the air raids towards the end of World War II but were rebuilt along almost identical lines in the postwar period. The park passed into the public domain two years after the war. The current garden, a multicultural masterpiece, is divided into a northern French and English section and a Japanese portion in the south.

Above A screen hanging in front of one of the garden's chrysanthemum pavilions. Purple is the imperial color in Japan and the chrysanthemum its imperial flower.
Left Pampas grass adds a naturalistic effect to the edge of the pond, a reminder that the plant once covered much of present-day Tokyo.

A popular spot for cherry blossom viewing in the spring, broad expanses of grassland are planted with over 20,000 trees, including some of the city's largest and oldest, from native oaks to ginkgos, platanus and towering cedars. There are approximately 1,500 cherry trees spread throughout the gardens. The *shidare-zakura* or weeping cherry blooms from late March to early April, the *somei-yoshino*, a common Tokyo tree, from early April onwards, and in late April, the *kanzan* cherry. The gardens cover an area of 58.3 hectares and have a circumference of 3.5 km.

The Japanese garden in the south contains many of the classic features associated with pond gardens, including stone lanterns, artificial pebble shores, traditional teahouses and pine trees. The pond in this meticulously landscaped area is transected by four bridges. Besides its design and ornamental features, the grounds provide a matchless setting for chrysanthemum viewing from late October through November. In many respects, the chrysanthemum is Japan's premier flower, at least in autumn, when its bloom comes to symbolize a quieter, more mature and contemplative season.

Above A spray of daffodils adds color to the edge of the Japanese garden pond.
Right The gardens and parkland are popular with Sunday painters.

Above Giant lily pads cultivated in the large, domed botanical garden.

Above One of over 75 varieties of cherry trees to bloom in the gardens.

Above A clump of imperial chrysanthemums concentrated into an English-style flower bed.

Right Adding a touch of rusticity to the gardens, the Raku-tei teahouse has several *yulan* magnolia trees in its grounds.

Above In full and splendid bloom, one of the many varieties of chrysanthemum at the autumn exhibition.

Koishikawa Shokubutsu-en

小石川植物園

Type **Botanical garden, Japanese garden**
Period **Late 17th century**
Commissioned by **Shogun Tsunayoshi**
Location **Hakusan, Bunkyo ward, Tokyo**

Above The graceful lines of the European-style Tokyo Medical School are a surprisingly harmonious match for this section of the formal garden.
Left Because it is an all-seasons garden, traces of late spring azaleas and early summer irises appear in a single perspective of the garden.

Within this spacious garden, behind its canopy of trees and the domes of its old greenhouses, the visitor experiences pleasant relief at having escaped the ring of sound that hums and clangs endlessly in busy Tokyo.

The garden traces its origins to 1684 when the *shogun* Tsunayoshi turned the estate into a center for the growing of medicinal herbs. It was also used to cultivate new varieties of plants and vegetables, such as sweet potato. A glimpse of the landscape of the original garden can be sensed in the remains of primary broad-leaved evergreens, conifers and deciduous forests found on the hilly slopes of the garden. Altogether, there are a staggering 7,000 species of herbaceous, subtropical and woody plants.

Paths flanked by bushes and thickets lead past a small grove of plum trees and a bed of irises to the Japanese garden proper. Complementing the rustic, naturalistic character of the garden, this bright, open area is less well maintained than other gardens in the city. In the summer, the pond is covered in yellow and red water lilies. These green, semi-rural grounds passed into the hands of Tokyo University in 1877. Botanical studies are still conducted and over a hundred species of herbs are grown here. The main building of

the old Tokyo Medical School, dating from 1876, stands at a slightly raised elevation above the pond. The structure, with its pink and white plaster façade and gleaming red portico, is an interesting hybrid of classical European, Renaissance and Romantic architecture, the plaster façade and portico reflecting a confluence of Meiji era tastes.

A path to the right of the Medical School rises through more woodland and an area of rhododendrons before reaching the medicinal herbal garden, where herbaceous plants dating from the Edo period are grown. The flat stones here were once used to dry medicinal herbs.

Unlike more formal gardens, this fusion of circulation and botanical garden is only casually tended, allowing nature a fuller expression. Even in the spacious Japanese section of the grounds, with its lily and sedge ponds, wisteria trellis, banks of lush azaleas and Sunday painters, an obvious lack of funds has precluded the mandatory army of gardeners seen in other gardens. A generous piece of land even at its founding, its value now in horticultural and human terms in space-depleted Tokyo cannot be overestimated.

Opposite Autumn eventually burns off the colors in the garden, but evergreens like pine remain.
Left A giant gingko tree in full flaming color, but the odor of its nuts, if approached too closely, can be surprisingly repellent.
Below left A narrow channel winds through this section of the garden, adding depth of perspective.
Right Russet autumn colors and the pampas grass of this section of the garden evoke the original wilderness of the area.
Below A carefully managed foreground of topiary contrasts with the more naturalistic rise of trees that form the backdrop to this portion of the garden.

Gardens of Ohara
三千院、宝泉院

Type **Temple gardens**
Period **16th-17th century**
Temple complex **Sanzen-in, Hosden-in**
Location **Raikoin-cho, Sanyo-ka, Ohara**

Above This small Zen temple sits in a clearing on the upper slopes of Sanzen-in, just above the hydrangea gardens.
Left A perfect blend of natural forest slope and landscape design in the upper sections of Sanzen-in.

The ancient Kyoto aristocracy who retired to Ohara coexisted in a simple but rarefied atmosphere with peasant farmers, high priests and monks. A sacred place for the faithful, ancient poets portrayed the village as a Buddhist Heaven on Earth. Surrounded by steep and mossy hills, broad rice-cultivating valleys, cryptomeria woods and rock-pitted rivers and brooks, the temple gardens of Ohara are landscapes created within the greater garden of nature itself.

Sanzen-in, standing in moss-covered grounds shaded by towering cryptomeria, is a sub-temple of Kyoto's grand Enryaku-ji. Soft flower-filled gardens, maples and massed hydrangea bushes replace the towering cedar woods that characterize the surroundings of the parent temple, blending in perfectly with the natural curvature of hill, forest line and mountain. The complex is an amalgam of buildings, some ancient, others more recently restored.

Genshin, the retired abbot of Enryaku-ji, had the first Amida Hall built here in 985. An advocate of the Tendai sect of Buddhism, he believed that even the unschooled masses could gain admittance to Amida's Pure Land paradise through prayer. The hall looks out over the Yuseien (Garden of Pure Presence), a less intricate, more natural garden with a bed of moss lying between the trunks of aged cryptomeria trees.

A circulation route leads the visitor across the verandahs of the Kyakuden reception chamber to the L-shaped Shuheki-in (Garden That Gathers Moss). The emerald corner of the garden at the right-angled viewing deck is an intensely massed compression of rising hedges and bushes that engages the eye before

Right The highly controlled forms of Shuheki-in (Garden That Gathers Moss) fuse surprisingly well with the more naturalistic woodland background.
Below The lily pond at Jikko-in, a delightful garden where green tea and a Japanese tea ceremony sweet are included in the admission fee.

visitors explore the open space of forest at the rear of the design. Paths through the forest above the temple wind through rhododendrons and bush clover, and a recent hydrangea garden created by a former abbot of Sanzen-in. The earth is acidic on the hillside here, so the flowers are a watercolor blue.

Nearby Hosen-in temple is distinguished by a magnificent 700-year-old pine at its entrance. The unusual form looks vaguely familiar, turning out to be clipped into the shape of Mount Fuji. The inner crane and turtle garden is framed like a painting or horizontal scroll by the pillars of the *tatami* room where visitors sit to contemplate the scene while sipping green tea served with a delicate Japanese sweet.

Top An unusual ring of stone slabs surrounds this water basin at Hosen-in.
Above Jikko-in is blessed with a number of rustic ornamental items, such as this moss-mottled *tsukubai* or water basin.

Left A careful stone and plant arrangement near the entrance to Hosen-in. **Right** The beauty of the setting of Ohara, a working agricultural village, is sometimes compared to a natural garden.

Left Trickling water from the slopes above Ohara cool down the garden precincts in the humid summer months.

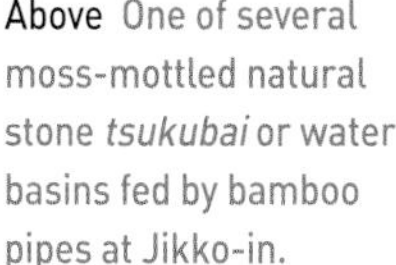

Above One of several moss-mottled natural stone *tsukubai* or water basins fed by bamboo pipes at Jikko-in.

Above A bronze Buddhist figure adds a touch of divinity to the elegant Jikko-in garden.

Kaku-ji Temple

勧修寺

Type **Pond and paradise garden**
Period **10th century**
Temple complex **Kaku-ji**
Location **Ono, Kyoto**

No garden can ever be entirely natural, but in terms of naturalism, over one millennium of weathering has served the landscape at Kaku-ji temple well. Conceived around AD 900, when the Miyaji family residence was converted to a temple, remnants of the original landscape design laid out on the outskirts of present-day Kyoto remain in the form of a stroll garden with a Himuro-ike (Icehouse Pond) at its center. Intended for leisurely boating, ice was taken from the surface of the pond every year on the second day of January and carried to the imperial court, where it was ritually presented and then examined. The success of the forthcoming grain harvest would be divined from the thickness of the ice.

The garden consists of four complementary layers. The first is a foreground of plantings along the edges of the pond; the design then

Above This stone lantern is surrounded by an evergreen shrub belonging to the Japanese cypress family *haibyakushin*. The bush is said to be over 750 years old.
Opposite The water lily section of the pond at Kaku-ji is best seen during the summer months.

Below The Horai Island at the center of the pond is a reference to the Chinese Isles of the Immortals.

Right The Buddhist world is created in the shaded garden border areas of Kaku-ji, where statues like this add to the air of antiquity.

alerts the eye to the densely cultivated Horai Island at the center of the pond. The composition of these two elements is sharpened by a tree line at the rear. The fourth level is a densely forested mountain. The absence of intrusive structures replaces the artifice that exists in many garden designs, with the sensation of viewing a completely natural setting with the lotus pond providing its visual focus.

The evolution of the lotus is understood as an allegory of spiritual growth. The flowers grow from the mud and sediment at the bottom of the shallow pond, a dark and viscous place that, in the anthropomorphic East, symbolizes the sullied, mortal world. As they grow, ascending from defilement, their leaves rise above the water line. With summer, the buds unfold into flowers of such exquisite beauty that they have become synonymous with divine perfection. The Chinese writer Zhou Tunyi interpreted its growth, the plant ascending like the soul "without contamination from the mud, reposing modestly above the clear water, hollow inside and straight without."

The pond's transfixing surface, the radiance issuing from the lotuses, creates a scene that has remarkable affinities to Amida's Western Paradise.

Left Two-story pagodas like this are the exception in Japan, where three and five tiers are the norm.

Above These decorative stone touches, including a granite ramp that resembles a pier, were a later addition to the garden.

Murin-an
無鄰菴

Type **Meiji era residential garden**
Period **Late 19th century**
Designer **Ogawa Jihei**
Location **Kusagawa-cho, Sakyo-ku, Kyoto**

Above The villa eaves and glass panels provide an ideal frame through which to view the garden. **Opposite** The water from this shallow stream is supplied by the Lake Biwa aqueduct, whose construction enabled several gardens in the Nanzen-ji district to be built during the Meiji and Taisho periods.

The completion in 1890 of a canal running from Lake Biwa to Kyoto had unexpected benefits for gardens. A plentiful supply of clear water created the opportunity to cultivate the land in the catchment area of Nanzen-ji temple into a site for prestigious villas with private gardens, many owned by wealthy businessmen from Osaka.

The man responsible for the majority of these landscape works was Ogawa Jihei (1860–1933), one of the foremost garden designers of the Meiji and Taisho periods. Garden writer Lorrain Kuck wrote of Ogawa gardens: "Their sole aim is to be as much like nature as possible—nature in its most enchanting and ideal moments."

The 3135 square meter garden is comparatively small, but transmits a sense of almost unlimited space and naturalism. The leafy, wooded area is a place to dwell, to shed the cumulative, extraneous elements of urban life. Its shallow head stream has much in common with glades throughout the temperate zone. Were it not for the telling way that rocks have been placed against the stream embankments and beside paths, the peculiarly Japanese aesthetic of the stone forms and the three-stepped waterfall, we could easily lose our cultural compass

terrain. The mesmerizing surfaces of the ponds flow slowly, reflecting slightly distorted images of the green overhead canopy, an effect similar to the view of the garden seen through some of the old, uneven windowpanes in the sliding doors of the villa.

Opposite A *naka-niwa* or courtyard garden at the center of the villa serves as a light well for the interior of the building.

Above The waters of the shallow, stone-littered stream create an almost pastoral mood in this wooded section of the garden.
Right Unusually tall trees form one of the wooded sides at the apex of the garden, where a fine view of the Higashiyama Hills can be glimpsed.

and mistake this dream world for a forest in the Dordogne or a wood in Gloucestershire, such is the meadow-like atmosphere of the grounds.

Close to the Higashiyama Hills, Ogawa adroitly requisitioned this natural feature as a backdrop, creating a V-shaped space between two small woods at the rear of the garden so that the distant hills could be captured and framed. Diverting water from the canal, Ogawa created a small filtering cascade, a shallow pond and a brook forming a fluid, liquid tracery over the gently sloping

CHAPTER 2

the modular garden

THE INTRODUCTION to the twelfth-century Chinese treatise, *The Cloud Forest Catalogue of Rocks*, by Du Wan contains the statement: "Within the proportions of a fist the beauty of a thousand cliffs can be assembled." This idea of the microcosm accommodating the macrocosm became a key principle in the composition of Japanese gardens, particularly the stone garden.

Miniaturization stemming from necessity, the natural limitations of space, became a design principle. The collapsing of physical space corresponded with the incorporation into gardens of highly compressed metaphoric and symbolic ideas, allusions to mythology, religion and an inquiry into man's relationship with nature.

With the introduction of Buddhism into Japan in the sixth century came the knowledge of a cosmology at the center of Indian Buddhist teachings. According to this vision of the universe, a huge mountain known as Mount Meru stood at the center of the world. Seven mountains, interspersed with oceans and seas possessed of magical or supernatural properties, formed concentric circles around the central peak. Humans inhabited an exterior zone, a salt ocean consisting of four continents and eight islands. The sea was encircled by an iron mountain range known as Cakravada. The motif of Mount Meru, known to Japanese as Shumisen, is often seen in gardens as a single upright stone supported by a concentric arrangement of lesser rocks. Another stone might be named after Fudo-myoo, the deity that purges the world of sin and guards the gates of hell.

Opposite The highly abstract gravel and sand garden at Kodai-ji, seen from the Kaisando, a hall where the temple's founder, Sanko Joeki, is enshrined.

Other stones were chosen to suggest desolate mountain ranges and shorelines or, by virtue of their colors and tones, to satisfy the demands of geomancy. In this way, primordial sculptural forms were imbued with sophisticated cultural and spiritual concepts.

The influence of Zen Buddhism in gardening reflects the interconnectedness of Japanese beliefs and art. This incorporation of cultural elements, ideas and forms is not generally found in Western gardens, which, however accomplished they may be, remain devoid of the deeper meanings and references integral to Japanese gardens. In this refined design milieu, teahouses, Buddhist statuary, stones inscribed with verse and flowers and plants with strong literary or mythological associations are placed into the garden scheme without creating the least suggestion of disharmony.

...one art means all art. —Nakane Kinsaku

Garden designers have frequently embraced other arts, immersing themselves in disciplines such as flower arranging, pottery and architecture. The master gardener Enshu Kobori was a renowned tea master; Sesshu was a respected painter and priest; the *haiku* and *waka* poet Matsunaga Teitoku designed gardens; the landscape iconoclast Shigemori Mirei was an accomplished calligrapher. This cross-cultural involvement predicated a degree of transference, the transposition of forms, styles and ideas to the Japanese garden.

In a Jade Garden

The Chinese, who first provided the Japanese with the plant, characterized green tea as liquid jade. Murata Shuko is generally credited with raising the tea ceremony to an art form by creating the *sukiya* or teahouse, an environment removed from private residencies and temples. However, it is the name Sen-no-Rikyu that most people associate with the refinement of style and the elements in the Japanese tea ceremony. Rikyu raised the level of the ceremony to such a degree that a cultured pastime became the "Way of Truth." His insistence on simplicity and the requisitioning of discarded objects for garden usage is in accord with the Japanese idea of *mottainai*, an abhorrence of waste.

Rikyu's disciple, Oribe Furuta, placed stones and trees in gardens, creating a greener, more aesthetically pleasing, albeit more contrived, tea environment. The aesthetic beauty and sparsity of the tea garden *roji* induce humility. A walk through physical space, the steps taken through the garden are also a walk through time. By interrupting sight lines, obscuring an overall view of the garden and stimulating expectations for subsequent views, the short paths of the *roji* slow down the visitor and add to a sense of spatial depth. Where more open designs sought to capture exterior elements in landscape in order to expand the interior, the tea garden turned inwards, eliminating views that would distract by creating a sequestered garden, one in which guests were made to feel they had stumbled upon the abode of a literate hermit situated in the depths of a forest.

Left An illustration from the Edo period manual, *Tsukiyama Teizoden* (Building Mountains and Making Gardens), provides a fine example of a design created from restricted space.

The merits of rural frugality are idealized and presented in surroundings that suggest the cultivated and the urbane. Striking a note of willing disassociation, the journey down the green, powdery paths of the tea garden, from the outer *roji* where guests wait to be invited, through the middle gate to the teahouse in the inner *roji* where the teahouse is located, is understood to be transformative, a passage between the world of evasive distractions and one of refined introspection.

Gardens of Light

If the *roji* was designed as a preliminary ritual to the tea ceremony, the small courtyard garden or *tsuboniwa* placed emphasis on viewing the garden from a fixed position, creating a composition of almost static tranquility. What they have in common is their transitional function, offering a detached privacy from the outside world. The courtyard garden represents a fusion of traditional aesthetics and functionalism, combining ventilation and lighting

alongside the refined pleasures of the Japanese garden.

Tsubo is the measurement of two adjacent *tatami* mats, *niwa* means garden. The *tsuboniwa* owes its conception to the design of the Chinese courtyard house, where residents are able to maintain privacy while opening their homes to the sky. The four sides of the dwelling or, in its temple incarnation, a quadrangle of walls and semi-exposed verandahs, revolve around a small space acting as the focus of a design in which architecture and nature are combined, and openness and enclosure are aligned in a garden that serves as a light well.

The gardens are hermetic, but never stifling. The judicious setting of a slim tree in the narrow confines of the garden invites the viewer to look upwards towards the sky, an effect that amplifies space. Emphasizing the importance of placement over size and scale, these scaled-down gardens embody many of the aims of contemporary urban design: space conservation, renewability, use of low-impact materials, aesthetic quality and durability.

Stone Enigmas, Zen Portals

In the *karesansui* (dry landscape garden), space is defined through inference, the reduction of mass, the essence of the garden suggested rather than revealed. Such economy of line implies the presence of the metaphysical lurking behind the material form of the garden. Stone gardens represent the most distilled form of Japanese garden design. In his 1477 treatise on gardens, the head priest at the Zen temple of Ryoan-ji wrote: "Thirty thousand leagues should be compressed into a single foot." Small, spatially accommodating and without recourse to water, the *karesansui* is the ultimate low-impact garden.

At the center of Zen is the contrast between stillness and fluidity. The mind cannot attain peace without stillness; yet the world is in perpetual, restless motion. If waves of sand represent movement in the garden, rocks stand for implacable immobility. In combining stillness and fluidity through the elimination of non-performing space, the essence of a garden is implied. Within the stillness and motion of the stone garden there is void and fullness. The garden is both empty and replete.

Although the expression Zen-tei (Zen garden) is rarely used in Japan, the idea of gardening as a method for practicing Zen is affirmed in the *Dream Dialogues*, where the monk and landscape designer Soseki Muso writes: "He who distinguishes between the garden and practice cannot be said to have found the true Way." Removing all non-essentials, leaving only stones, gravel and a little greenery, these gardens attempt to draw us closer to the more transcendent qualities of existence. By condensing the universe to the most finite scale, the priests, monks and acolytes who served at Zen temples could identify its essence and, in the process, find their own "original nature."

Profound Beauty

The spirit of Zen is manifest in ways as countless as the sands of the Ganges. —Ikkyu

Consistent with the higher realms of Zen is the aesthetic known as *miyabi*. A Heian period term, it implies a refined sensitivity capable of apprehending the more profound aspects of beauty. Those who are able to appreciate the patina of a garden wall, the discoloration of a bronze Buddha or the grain of a garden rock are privy to the spiritual reality underlying objects.

The preference for asymmetrical balance over symmetry, the notion that equilibrium results in disorder and disorganization while imbalance is intrinsically energizing, is manifest in Japanese stone garden design. Rocks are used to steady and transfix the garden, to still motion and to add depth. The bluish tint of distant mountains set at the rear of a garden, an effect achieved through the use of plants and upright rocks, can add authority and spatial depth. The use of color to heighten depth can be seen in the dry landscape garden of Daisen-in, a Kyoto temple, where the garden uses camellias to great effect. The dark, glossy evergreen leaves, clipped into mountain forms, stand at the back of the garden's dry waterfall composition. The technique creates the impression of mountains receding into the distance. The white rear wall behind the camellias suggests banks of clouds, a color neutral infinity.

These highly modular landscapes possess a philosophical and spiritual content that is rare, even unknown, in the gardens of the world. In their mastery of space, of nature transmuted into art, the Japanese garden realizes a state in which the external world no longer holds sway.

Opposite The shape of a firebird dominates the southern section of the garden at Sekizo-ji.

Chishaku-in
智積院

Type **Pond viewing garden**
Period **Late 17th century**
Designer **Sen-no-Rikyu (attributed)**
Temple complex **Chishaku-ji**
Location **Higashikawara-cho, Higashiyama-ku, Kyoto**

This Kyoto temple, located in the south-east of the city, belongs to the influential Chizan School of the Buddhist Shingon sect. The garden dates from 1674, though the present landscape was probably created in 1682 after a temple fire. Attributed to the great tea master Sen-no-Rikyu, there is no actual evidence to support that claim. More verifiable is the fact that the priest Sosei rebuilt the garden in 1674.

The mountain Lu-shan in China is said to have been the inspiration for the garden, whose pond is configured as if it were a river winding its way through a rocky terrain. Scale and perspective are used to great effect in the southern part of the garden, where they create the illusion of deep space. Perspective depth is expanded by tapering the edges of the pond and its banks. A lantern stands above the shrubbery of

Above An imperial touch to the curtain design at the slightly removed private entrance at the rear of the temple.
Opposite The main garden and embankments viewed from inside the tranquil *shoin*, a place of deep repose.

Above This distinctly shaped *furisode* water basin adds sculptural form to the foreground of the main garden. **Above right** Colored banners add visual interest to the long, narrow perspectives, which are a feature of the verandah abutting sections of the garden.

the eastern rise, its scale diminished as if it were being viewed from a far distance.

The design of the main garden is striking for the way the pond's water flows under the main buildings. The verandah of the *shoin* is cantilevered over the carp-filled water in the style of a *tsuridono* or fishing pavilion. Divided into sections, the main portion of the garden lies to the east of the *shoin*, from which a verandah allows an excellent viewing position. A higher compositional aesthetic is achieved in the arrangement of rocks and clipped shrubs that ascend beyond the pond to a tree line, a highly effective space-enlarging effect.

The focal point of the garden is a waterfall placed between large rocks and shrubbery on the eastern slope. This was originally a dry fall. Water now flows over a grooved rock into the pond. From particular viewing positions the garden can only be observed in carefully framed sections rather than in its entirety.

The compositionally weaker north side of the *shoin* is a late Edo or early Meiji addition. Open corridors zigzag around the temple buildings, providing viewing stages for minor but tastefully conceived sub-gardens that include a dry landscape design.

Vivid paintings on the inner walls of the *shoin* of maples and cherries by

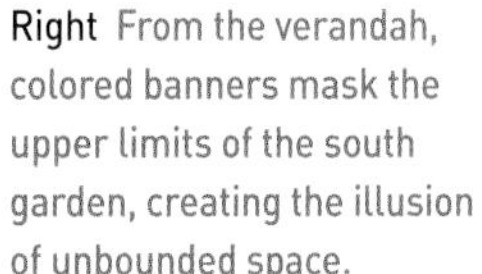

Right From the verandah, colored banners mask the upper limits of the south garden, creating the illusion of unbounded space.
Far right Typically, water basins are complemented with an ensemble of rocks and small stones or gravel.
Below The waterfall in front of the *shoin* provides the main focal point of the south garden. This was originally dry, but now water trickles through the massed landscape above.

the master artist Hasegawa Tohaku and his eldest son complement the garden's creative interpretation of nature. *Fusuma-e* (paintings conceived on the paper surfaces of sliding door panels) are the work of the Kyoto artist Domoto Insho.

A more recent work, adding depth to the consideration of nature, is a black-ink screen painting of the four seasons by Tabuchi Toshio, dedicated to the temple in 2008.

Ryutan-ji Garden

龍潭寺

Type **Temple and pond garden**
Period **Early to late 17th century**
Designer **Enshu Kobori (attributed)**
Temple complex **Ryutan-ji**
Location **Inasa-gun, Shizuoka prefecture**

Right The small water lily pond that forms a fluid transition between the temple's viewing veranda and the garden proper takes the shape of the Chinese character *kokoro*, meaning "heart." **Left** Complex topiary and grass banks help to soften the effect of rocks made from red chert, a local mountain stone.

The authorship of important gardens in Japan is often disputed. The name Enshu Kobori (1579–1647) is associated with an almost impossible number of gardens in Japan.

Some landscape authorities have suggested that the current garden at Ryutan-ji dates from 1676, when the main hall was reconstructed following a fire. If not an original Enshu masterwork, the garden, with its singular use of stones and curvaceous hillocks that combine to form an intensely compact design, would appear to be directly influenced by his style.

Topiary is an important element in garden design, and a hallmark of Enshu gardens. As a landscape feature it takes its place in Japanese gardening alongside miniature stone pagodas, lanterns, water basins and millstones, the symbolic or merely referential ornamental elements that grace many Japanese gardens. The difference between

Right A solitary pine stands at the top of the eastern section of the garden. Pines have always been associated with mountains or shorelines in Japan.

stone ornamentation and topiary is that the latter is a living shape, an organic form. Unless the trimming is done with great skill, the end results can look extremely artificial. Unlike Western topiary, Japanese *karikomi* seeks to create softer, more fluid shapes and lines. Small-scale topiary, low and broad, with sides that taper almost imperceptibly above ground level, creates a tension akin to the relationship between surfaces and drops of water or mercury.

The configuration of a narrow, lily-filled pond laying north of the main hall resembles the ideogram for "heart." Acting as the under frame for three symbolic mountain ranges covered in grass and azalea bushes, the imagery of steep valleys is provided by dry waterfall rock formations.

The middle range of the garden has a *kamejima* (turtle island) at its foot, while the western range has a *tsurujima* (crane island). A Horai Island stands between them. Resolving the design and acting as its focal point is a *sanzonzeki* stone grouping just below the summit of the middle range. A meditation rock on the southern bank, and two guardian stones at each end of the garden provide extra interest and internal symmetry.

Left A stone pagoda adds interest to the upper rear area of the garden.
Below The so-called Western and Middle Mountain Range rise sharply from the pond, their compression giving the effect of depth in what is actually a fairly shallow plot of available land.

Toji-in

等持院

Type Pond and island garden
Period 14th century, present structures early 19th century
Designer Soseki Muso (attributed)
Temple complex Toji-in
Location Kitamachi, Kita-ku, Kyoto

Above The lichen-mottled rim of a water basin adds to the sense of easily acquired antiquity, which is possible in Kyoto's humid summer months. **Opposite** A series of tea-rooms floats above a solid structure of rock, greenery and water, creating a sinuous fusion of architecture and gardening.

Established in 1341 by Ashikaga Takauji, Toji-in temple remained the family's principal place of worship during a span of fifteen Ashikaga shoguns. The gardens are attributed to Soseki Muso, its first abbot, but this remains under dispute. The older east pond, named Shinjichi (Heart-shaped Pond), was probably dug around this time, but the Fuyo-chi (Lotus Pond) is more likely an Edo period creation.

A surprisingly overlooked Kyoto garden, its precisely aligned banks of intensely cultivated topiary blend with low trees and a small teahouse that seems to float on billowing clouds of azalea. Rocks lend stability to the garden, ensuring that the effervescent topiary remains earthbound. The ascending banks of evergreens, reflected in a pond, are seen from a path that changes levels and the corresponding view of the garden.

The rustic teahouse, known as Seiren-tei, stands at the top of an

escarpment held in place by countless rocks and stepping-stones set firmly in the earth. Paths meander up and over this raised section of the garden, providing views of the pond and temple buildings. The complex arrangement of stones, paths and low bushes effortlessly connect the two garden levels, leaving the teahouse to "float" above the composition.

The elevated corridors and viewing verandahs of the temple buildings afford different perspectives of the garden. Creaking wooden planks speak of age, the tread of feet. An important tea ceremony location, the tearooms are situated like galleries, offering framed images of the garden.

Overshadowed by nearby world garden icon Ryoan-ji, and the landscape at Ninna-ji temple complex, Toji-in is never oppressively busy, which is fitting, as it was built for tranquility. Old trees, still water, winding paths and beds of moss characterize the neighboring east garden. The spatial brilliance of Toji-in is defined by its resolving of contrasting garden forms into a fluid and unified single space.

Above Attributed to the Buddhist prelate Soseki Muso, Toji-in is one of Kyoto's most undervalued gardens, receiving little more than a trickle of visitors.

Below The classic *sanzonseki* stone triad may either represent mythical Mount Sumeru or the Buddha flanked by two disciples.

Left This carefully designed stone corner suggests the ascent of a mountain range.
Opposite above left Although they are generally devoid of implicit meanings, stone lanterns, when well placed, can be highly appropriate ornamentations in a traditional garden.
Opposite below left The pink blossom of the *saru-suberi* (crepe myrtle) tree adds a dash of color to Toji-in during the high summer months.

Kodai-ji Garden

高台寺

Type **Temple pond and hill garden**
Period **Early 17th century**
Designer **Enshu Kobori**
Temple complex **Kodai-ji**
Location **Gion, Kyoto**

Above Kaisando, the Founder's Hall, has been designated an Important Cultural Property.
Left A common motif in dry landscape gardens, the cone ringed by gravel ripples symbolizes purity.

The seemingly ubiquitous garden designer Enshu Kobori is credited with replacing an existing garden with the current landscape in this interesting mix of temple buildings and teahouses at Kodai-ji.

If you arrive early, just as the garden opens, you will walk along paths freshly sprinkled with water, a traditional courtesy, a sign of respect to guests or visitors. You may also see workers watering the garden. The small rituals, chores and code signage humanize gardens and deepen our interest. The *moriseki* placed at the entrance to one of the garden's teahouses, for example, is a dark stone tied with hemp that signifies non-admittance to this section of the grounds.

Two teahouses designed by the tea master Sen-no-Rikyu have been moved into the garden, and are now Important Cultural Properties. The aquatic section of the garden is divided into the eastern Garyu Pond and the western Engetsu Pond. The pond to the east of Kaisando (the Founder's Hall) is breached by a bridge called Rosenro (Tower Boat Way). In the classic manner, the northern segment of the pond contains a *kameshima* (turtle island), the southern section a *tsurujima* (crane island).

Right This cascading cherry tree at the rear of the main hall contrasts with the stark simplicity of the dry landscape expanse.
Below The Otama-ya, another Important Cultural Property, is a sanctuary containing priceless wooden images and lacquer art.

The idea of paths, stone steps and verandahs designed to provide different views of the garden is a Japanese design motif offering diverse perspectives on the main themes and central concepts of a garden. Whether by design or by felicitous coincidence, the patterns in the wooden planks of the verandah facing the temple's stone garden replicate the wave shapes raked in the sand, the knots in the timber and the stones in the garden.

Situated on the slopes of Mount Shuho, part of the undulating Higashiyama Hills, the visitor is barely aware of the boundary between the garden and the forested terrain beyond. The use of captured scenery creates a spatial dimension that far exceeds the material parameters.

Above The simplest of dry landscape gardens appreciated from the main hall of Kodai-ji temple.

Sekizo-ji
石像寺

Type **Dry landscape garden**
Period **1972**
Designer **Shigemori Mirei**
Temple complex **Sekizo-ji**
Location **Tanba-Takeda, Ichijima-cho, Hyogo prefecture**

Gardens are art, an avant-garde art.
—Shigemori Mirei

Above A tiger shape erupts out of the white gravel of the west section of the garden. **Opposite** The four quarters of the garden are clearly divided into sections representing turtle, dragon, firebird and dragon figures.

Most stone gardens of importance are located near the centers of culture. The garden at Sekizo-ji temple, completed in 1972, is an exception. The design stands in magnificent solitude in the courtyard of a hillside temple reached by climbing a set of stone steps. The abode of dragonflies and occasional lizards in the summer, Sekizo-ji is one of those gardens that deserves more visitors, but is better off for not having them. Here, landscape iconoclast Shigemori Mirei created a unique design that challenges the limits of the stone garden.

The current temple was built close to an imposing *iwakura*—stones believed to be the site for the congregation of gods. Inspired by the stones, Shigemori's garden is a modern habitat for ancient deities.

Based on the Chinese concept of *shisin soo*, the four gods that guard the heavenly directions, each deity is represented by a cluster of color-coded rocks. Associated with the color black, the tortoise, guardian of water, symbolizes the North. Stones arranged in the form of a tortoise are accordingly placed on a rectangle of black pebble. The East segment represents the dragon, guardian of

Left The dragon is the guardian of the earth, so the designer has placed the stone arrangement on a bed of dark blue gravel, the color associated with this figure.

the earth. Associated with the color blue, elongated stones are placed over a bed of blue gravel. A large plane of reddish sand occupies the South, symbol of the phoenix, guardian and protector of fire. A stone arrangement in the form of the firebird spreading its wings dominates this portion of the garden. Resembling the outline of a tiger, an arrangement of pale rocks represents the West. The domain of the tiger, the wind guardian, is assigned the color white.

Bamboo rods have been organized across the fence behind the red phoenix stone arrangement. These read *shishin* or "four gods," the main theme of the garden. Another Chinese character, reading *seki* (stone), stands close to the bell tower and is an allusion to the *iwakura*, source of the temple's origin.

In Shigemori's concept, the *kami* descend from the *iwakura* on the hill above the temple, enter the north point of the garden and move in a counterclockwise direction from one grouping to the next until the four gods engage in a circular dance. Employing four tones of gravel and eschewing the convention of imitating natural landscapes, Sekizo-ji signals the advent of a garden of rare geometrical abstraction in Japan.

Left A side garden at the temple affords views of borrowed scenery. The stones are blue schist, a favorite of the designer.

Above The phoenix stone configuration is laid out over rust-colored sand, the perfect match for the protector of fire.
Right Individualized stone paving helps to divide the garden into four symbolic sections.

CHAPTER 3

landscape gardens

ALMOST ALL JAPANESE GARDENS, from the barest, most minimal rock formations to the lush and sinuously contoured depict some form of landscape.

In a pre-enactment of later designs, Nara and Heian period gardens created rescaled versions of landscapes located in remote parts of the country into compressed tableaux of vibrant nature. Popular re-creations included the islands of the Inland Sea, the coast at Sumiyoshi, and Tamatsushima in Kii Province.

With the rare exception of landscape gardens like Motsu-ji in the northern city of Hiraizumi, or Nara's older, meticulously reconstructed To-in, only the excavated foundations of such gardens have survived to the present day. The closest existing form to these earlier gardens of the imagination is the Edo period (1600–1868) Japanese stroll garden.

Opposite Suizen-ji Joju-en in Kumamoto is one of the finest examples of Edo period stroll garden landscaping in Japan.

After centuries of sporadic warfare, in which many gardens were destroyed or vandalized, the Edo era rapidly unified the country under the authority of a powerful shogunate. Despite the intrusive controls and checks, it was the prelude to a long period of relative social stability. Forbidden from spending funds on enlarging their military arsenals, the wealthy, once powerful nobles and *daimyo* (the lords of the capital and provinces) now engaged in harmless forms of rivalry as they vied with each other over who possessed the finest art collections, brocades and tea gardens. These latter, exquisitely designed enclosures, the pinnacle of any sophisticated household, grew in scale over time until groupings of teahouses coagulated into sprawling grounds that provided the eventual setting for the Edo stroll garden.

The modern term for these gardens, *kayushiki teien*, stroll or excursion gardens, hints at the function of large landscapes in which guests were invited to take a leisurely meander through a number of scenes that would be akin to a cultural itinerary. The entrepreneurial flair, brash and brio of the socially despised but newly moneyed merchant class of the Edo period, combined with the classical, Confucian education of the aristocracy, resulted in gardens whose character was both sophisticated and playful.

The Themed Garden

In common with landscape painting, the stroll garden pays tribute to natural forms. A key guideline in the *Sakuteiki* admonishes gardeners, before they commence work, to "Reflect on the famous places of scenic beauty found throughout the land." *The Illustrations For Designing Mountain, Water, and Hillside Field Landscapes* by the fifteenth-century priest Zoen, is even more explicit when its says: "The landscape garden mirrors nature. It is, therefore, said that in every circumstance we must return to the two words, natural habitat."

Commissioned works or *kaiyushiki-teien* were designed by professional gardeners called *niwa-shi*. Representational, the gardens cleverly mirrored concepts and settings, both real and imaginary, found in Chinese and Japanese history and literature. Visitors followed a route that featured *meisho* or "famous sights." These landscape compendiums obviated the need to undertake long and arduous journeys on foot over mountain passes, on horseback or by boat that often involved months away from home.

Though the visual references may elude the non-Japanese, these secular gardens, imitating the outer forms of nature, are relatively simple in their conception, representing the style and taste of the period. The occasional addition of Buddhist statuary and miniature Shinto shrines is largely decorative. Images and scenery have largely replaced symbolism. Devoid of the tensions inseparable from the stone garden, *kaiyushiki-teien* are pleasure gardens whose radiations are more sensual than spiritual or cerebral.

The Sequential Garden

Whereas the stone garden restricts our gaze by designating a fixed vantage point, one that reveals the garden in its framed entirety, the stroll garden takes the opposite approach by offering only partial glimpses while following a prescribed circulatory layout. The complete garden is rarely seen in one view. The more linear axis of the stone garden is replaced with the *miegakure* ("hide-and-reveal") technique, one that freed designers from spatial limitations.

In unfolding space, highlighting panels one at a time, enlarging our perception of scale, motion and framing, are crucial. The stroll garden is designed to make the visitor stop, pause and observe. This form of benign manipulation is intended to startle the viewer with fresh and engaging compositions at every turn. In the arranging of panels containing singular visual effects, the stroll garden becomes both a *mise-en* scene of nature and a lexicon of Japanese culture.

Above Engetsu-kyo, Ritsurin-koen's graceful Bridge of the Round Moon.
Opposite An Edo period garden manual demonstrates one aspect of water flow management and the placement of man-made structures in large landscapes.

In this art of concealment and revelation, of contrast and inference, the proximate is favored over the distant, using stepping-stones and paths to focus visitors on specific garden tableaux. Foregoing the axial in favor of paths that meander, perspectives that heighten space, and a sense of arrival and recommencement, the visitor is stimulated at each turn as new vistas and seasonal colors unfold and are then withdrawn.

Perspective is manipulated to maximize space and time. Measured progress is made from confined to open ground, shadowy gloom to bright light, water margins to high ground. The undulating shoreline of the pond is often interrupted by a tree, hill or rock, forcing observers to apply their powers of imagination to supply the missing landscape features beyond the immediate view, accessed along more winding paths and hidden boundaries that create an impression of infinite space.

Teleporting Space
Letting the mountain
Move into the garden
A summer room
—Basho

The technique of appropriating scenery and other natural features into the confines of gardens was practiced as early as the Heian period, though it was not conceptualized as the *shakkei* or "borrowed view" method. By the Kamakura period (1185–1333) we hear of the retired emperors Kameyama and Gofukakusa traveling by ox-drawn carriages to Fushimi Palace in order to enjoy the view from its garden of the Uji River and nearby hills ablaze with autumn colors.

The method was established in the later Muromachi era (1333–1568). The term *shakkei* appears for the first time in China (as *chieh-ching*) in the beginning of the seventeeth century, but not until the nineteenth century in Japan. Gardeners in Kyoto began to use the expression *ikedori* ("capturing alive") to describe the process of incorporating a borrowed landscape into gardens. The concept accords with the Chinese painter and garden creator Ji Cheng's advocacy in the *Yuan ye* (Manual of Garden Design), published in 1634, that "skill in landscape design is shown in the ability to 'follow' the lie of the land and 'borrow from' the existing scenery."

Shakkei, though largely naturalistic, are often subject to space and perspective management, with undesirable elements in the exterior view eliminated or recomposed with the help of clay walls topped with tile or bushes grown and clipped into forms designed to enhance or conceal. A view of a distant mountain is often captured by viewing it through a grouping of trees such as evergreen oaks, red pines and zelkova, which help to modify a grand vista. Symbiosis is, nevertheless, achieved, the removed and the immediate nourishing each other. A distant view of nature is enticed into the garden, creating an art composition.

The Well-Shaped World

To create thoroughly grounded, coordinated compositions, *The Illustrations* advises designers to keep faith with the raw materials used in gardens, to establish a correspondence between the original site and the new one, stating:

> *When setting rocks, make their geological zones the model ... setting rocks from deep mountains in the deep mountains of the garden, rocks from the hills and fields in the hills and fields, rocks from fresh water shores on the fresh water shores, and rocks taken from the seashore on the seashore.*

Left Azalea bushes at Rikugi-en, one of Tokyo's oldest garden landscapes.

We know the garden is conceived, but a successful landscape conveys the sense of everything belonging in its natural setting, even when those elements, like topiary, are conspicuously contrived. In Japanese, *karikomi* (topiary) has rather different connotations. Hedges, trees and shrubbery are still clipped and shaped, but the intentions are quite distinct. Forms are created as integral ingredients in the harmony of the garden and, in some instances, to complement the natural landscapes that lay beyond the garden boundaries.

A well-established feature of Japanese gardens, the practice was raised into an art form in the Momoyama (1568–1600) and Edo periods. Enshu Kobori (1579–1647), a garden designer and arbiter of the tea ceremony, a man of immense talent and creativity, is often described as Japan's first landscape architect. A prolific designer, he introduced the concept of *okarikomi*, in which dense plantings were clipped into the shapes of mountains, clouds, tree lines and, in their most abstract form, wave patterns. In this highly representative world, where trees are shaped to suggest forest depths and floating clouds, it is possible to come across the form of Mount Fuji sculpted from a single tree.

In European gardens, where rectangles, cubes and spheres are common, topiary tends towards the formal and geometric. The Japanese garden aesthetic favors flowing, organic shapes grown at low levels or in intense groupings, attempts to replicate landscape. Unlike gardens such as those at Vaux-le-Vicomte in France, where trees and hedges are designed as idealized, living sculptures, forms in the Japanese context *are* the garden, with the surroundings reduced to auxiliary elements. Like an undulating dragon, the power of this living topiary comes from the illusion of movement, of creating organic rhythms and dialogs within the garden.

In the circulation garden, topiary is one more means of expressing the ultimate purpose of all Japanese gardens—the search for the essence of landscape.

Sengan-en

仙巌園

Type **Stroll garden**
Period **Mid-17th century**
Designer **Shimazu Mitsuhisa**
Location **Kagoshima, Kagoshima prefecture**

Left The Okinawan style Bogakuro Pavilion dates from the nineteenth century, when guests and dignitaries from the kingdom of Ryukyu would come to pay their respects to the head of the region's Shimazu clan.
Right Stone steps leading up through a bamboo grove at the rear of the garden.

Mitsuhisa, the nineteenth lord of the powerful Shimazu clan, began building Sengan-en in 1658. The grounds were extensively restored in 1830 and again in 1844. Its sea-facing promenades suggest a park or pleasure garden, the grounds climbing up a wooded hillside bisected by a ravine above the harbor.

The garden is renowned for its stone lanterns. The most imposing, the Lion Stone Lantern, was designed by Sengan-en's head gardener, Oda Kisanji, in 1884. The lantern's coping stone equals the width of eight *tatami* mats and was once used as a wave-breaker at nearby Iso Beach.

Bogakuro, an airy structure hinting at the southern climate of the garden, resembles an open-sided gazebo. Presented by the king of the Ryukyu islands (present-day Okinawa) during the reign of the 19th Lord Mitsuhisa, it was used to host representatives from the semi-tropical islands. The floor

Above This stone lantern, supposedly in the shape of a lion, has become a distinctive feature of the garden.
Above right This sun-drenched garden is rich in evergreen cycads or *Cycas revolute*, an ancient plant dating back, in some instances, 240 million years.

is covered with 273 pieces of tile in a design copied from ceramics at the Ching Dynasty E Fang Gong Palace.

Stone lanterns, dry waterfalls, clipped bushes and hedges stand in for an almost complete lack of large trees in the main garden, where flat and sloping lawns are placed between rock clusters. On the instructions of the 27th Lord Nariaki, Chinese characters of one meter long were engraved on the rock face to the rear of the garden in April 1814. Some 3,900 workers, using bamboo scaffolding, spent three months completing the task. Engraving large characters on rock cliffs, a common Chinese practice, is rare in Japan.

The severed head of Sakurajima, an active volcano dominating Kagoshima Bay, acts as captured scenery, the effect of its massive outline and rising plumes of black ash only slightly marred by a line of electricity standards just beyond the garden's sea-facing border.

Left Mount Senjinkan rises beyond the garden. The three ideograms inscribed on the stone monument reach a height of 11 meters.
Below The elegant Bogakuro Pavilion frames a view of Sengan-en and the distant volcano of Sakurajima.

Koraku-en

後楽園

Below left Stone steps leading to the man-made hill of Yuishinzan.
Right Enyo-tei House, used as a guest reception area for important clan members, commands a fine view of all the major features of the garden.

Type **Stroll garden**
Period **Late 17th century**
Commissioned by **Ikeda Tsunamasa**
Location **Okayama City, Okayama prefecture**

Themes may be repeated in an infinite variety of ways in the Japanese garden, but designs are always in some way inimitable. The Koraku-en (Garden for Taking Pleasure Later) in Okayama City accurately reflects the directives contained in the eleventh century garden manual, the *Sakuteiki*, which inveighs designers to "Think of the finest natural landscapes you have seen, select those that you find most inspiring, and adapt them to your plan."

Among the landscape garden's cleverly contrived effects is an artificial thicket, whose miniature valleys, mountains and waterfalls are said to be modeled after scenery along the ancient Kiso Road. Okayama Castle, just beyond the perimeters of the garden, forms part of its borrowed view. The presence of the fortress reminds us that features requisitioned from outside a garden's perimeters do not have to be natural forms.

Facing the imposing upper stories of the castle, this large 13.3 hectare garden sits on the northern bank of the Asahi River. Built on an island between the river and a developed city strip, it is an ideal location if one discounts the traffic sounds and most of the high-rise buildings. The castle, the only high-rise of any importance, is an integral part of the garden.

The chirp of cicadas and the cries of red-crested cranes kept near the entrance carry across the garden. The central pond, Sawa-no-ike (Marsh Pond), contains three islands and is

Above This low boat shelter near Naka-no-shima Island is made in the traditional manner from thatch and bamboo, materials that perfectly complement the garden environment.
Above right The Yatsuhashi Bridge, with irises growing nearby, is a common theme in stroll gardens, and is a reference to the *azumakudari* chapter of an ancient narrative called the "Tale of Ise."

purported to replicate the scenery around Lake Biwa near Kyoto. Groves of plum, cherry, maple and pine, a rice field and a tea plantation, are ranged around the open center of water. An artificial mountain called Yuishisan rises above banks of azalea hedges, offering magnificent views of the grassy parkland.

Lawns have been popular features of Japanese gardens since the Edo period, but rarely on the scale seen here. Viewing the grassy expanses at Koraku-en as the garden's main feature may be counter-productive, however, inviting comparisons with the manicured perfection of gardens in England and France. Here it is better to stress the indigenous garden features, of which there are an abundance. Today, the garden serves as an events space, doubling for festivals, community activities and cultural performances, a multipurpose function that exploits the spatial possibilities of this large tract of land.

Though much of the landscape had to be rebuilt after severe damage in World War II, its scale and proportions remain remarkably faithful to the original feudal garden, which has been purportedly restored on the basis of paintings and diagrams owned by the Ikeda family.

Left A view of Yuishinzan Hill beyond fields of lotuses and rice.

Right An old tinted postcard depicts a bridge passing over Kayo-no-ike, a pond that is now full of white lotuses.

Right A meandering stream passes in front of the Enyo-tei House.

Right A bright, open garden, Koraku-en is known for its large expanses of grass. The planting of lawns first began in the Edo period and was further developed in the Meiji era.

Shuizen-ji Joju-en

水前寺

Type **Stroll garden**
Period **Early 17th century**
Commissioned by **Hosokawa Tadatoshi**
Location **Kumamoto, Kumamoto prefecture**

A raft of souvenir and snack shops crowd the approach to Joju-en. A postman rides his motorbike into the grounds, children with paper fans kick up gravel and noisily chase after pigeons; souvenir, tea and snack stands are positioned throughout the garden. Joju-en is an example of all that is right and wrong with gardens in the modern age.

Laid out by the Hosokawa family in 1632 to serve as the grounds for a detached villa, this classic stroll garden embodies the twin characteristics of refinement and playfulness. Its representational features include scenes from the 53 stages of the old Tokaido highway, and the outline of Lake Biwa near Kyoto. A remarkably realistic, grass-covered Mount Fuji is a fine example of *shukkei*, miniaturizations of natural scenery.

The centerpiece of the garden, the mountain image stands above undulating, grassy knolls rising from the edge of the pond. Perspective is enlarged by systematically reducing the scale of the miniature trees planted on its slopes, larger trees at the base, smaller trees near the summit. In this way, infinite distances are inferred. Adding to the illusion of a natural landscape is the *sawatobi-ishi* or "stepping-stones over a marsh," a line of flat stones stretched across

Above The garden's celebrated miniature Mount Fuji, a much-replicated theme in gardens that sought to represent famous sights in Japan.
Opposite From the 400-year-old teahouse on the west side of the pond, stepping-stones connect two of the three islands in the pond.

Above One of two stone bridges that represent some of the original elements of the garden. **Above center** An old sepia tinted postcard represents a scene almost identical to the present day. To the left, the *torii* gate to Izumi Shrine can be seen. **Right** Well-appointed teahouses often command the best views of Japanese gardens.

the pond just beneath the slopes. The quality of rocks and stones in the garden, and their placement settings in general, is not high. The strength of the garden rests in its contours and lines, the sinuous linkage of sections. There is something playful about Joju-en, the feeling of an early model for theme attraction parks, modified by the design affectations of a master garden.

Its compromised seriousness suggests a space that is as much about recreation as art. The photographer Herbert G. Ponting sensed this when he visited the garden in the late Meiji era, recalling in his 1911 chronicle, *In Lotus-Land Japan*, how he enjoyed a cone of shaved ice and fruit syrup there under a pine tree in August, a famously humid month. Ponting noted groups of adult men bathing in the central pond, and small children "paddling in the water and scampering over the grasses." Despite the distractions, Joju-en remains a fine, even eminent circulation garden.

Above Complex landscaping and space management at the center of the garden.

Ritsurin-koen

栗林公園

Type **Stroll garden**
Period **Mid-18th century**
Commissioned by **Matsudaira daimyos**
Location **Takamatsu, Kagawa prefecture**

Above A traditional moon-shaped window adds elegance and ventilation to one of the rooms inside the Kikugetsu-tei teahouse.
Left A magisterial view of the south pond or Nanko can be enjoyed from the Hiraiho hilltop, a man-made mound.

The old pines are full of poems
—the Zen monk Ryokan

One of the finest *daimyo* stroll gardens in Japan, a pond garden once existed here at the base of Shiunsan (Purple Cloud Mountain) during the Momoyama period. The garden was expanded over several generations of the Matsudaira clan during the Edo period, reaching its current proportions of 750,000 square meters in 1745.

It seems a disservice to merely call it a park. This is landscaping at its most supremely accomplished. The designation was applied in the Meiji period, when private feudal estates were requisitioned and, in some instances, opened to the public in imitation of Western parks.

Less an example of nature confronting the artifice of a garden, Ritsurin-koen represents a near seamless blending of the two, especially seen in views across pine trees to Mount Shiun and at the point where the Sekiheki (Red Wall) cliff angles down to the inner channel waters of Seiko Lake. Quite where the mountain ends and the garden commences is not clear.

There is a dream-like atmosphere at the Kikugetsu-tei (Moon Scooping Pavilion) teahouse in the older southern section of the garden, its main viewing room floating above the green surface of Nanko Lake, the garden's South Pond, where water ripples are reflected on the tearoom ceiling. In this tranquil section of the garden, an abundance of unusual stones and Judas trees adds interest.

Above The interior of the Kikugetsu-tei, a teahouse that is still used to give lessons in the tea ceremony.

Right A barge moored in a quiet inlet of Seiko Lake, an expanse of water at the rear of the garden, beneath Mount Shiun.

Left The garden is one of the most intensely planted pine landscapes in the country, with varieties and forms including red and black pines, *byobu-matsu*, a pine network that resembles a classical Japanese screen, and *hako-matsu*, a pine trained into a tall, box-like hedge.

The cubic form of the distinctive bushes and hedges at Ritsurin-koen is known as *hako-zukuri* or "box-making" topiary. Rare pines achieve a stylistic innovation in the so-called *byobumatsu* series of trees, whose form is named after folding screens (*byobu*), often decorated with images of gnarled pines and plum trees. The trees, tightly fused, create an undulating green exterior supported by a complex basketwork of branches. They are a fine example of nature inspiring horticultural art.

A supremely successful work of landscape design, Ritsurin-koen represents a matchless blend of naturalism and artifice.

Top An old postcard depicts buildings still standing today, though their present function as a souvenir shop and for regional promotion may have changed.
Above Crossing a lotus pond, Eitai-bashi bridge remains much the same today as it appears in this Taisho period postcard.
Right Kikugetsu-tei teahouse seen from one of several pine mounds distributed throughout the garden.

Rikugi-en

六義園

Type **Stroll garden**
Period **Late 17th century**
Designer **Yanagisawa Yoshiyasu**
Location **Honkomagome, Bunkyo-ku, Tokyo**

Above Stone lanterns were first introduced to gardens in the late sixteenth century by tea masters, but became collector's items in the later Meiji era.
Opposite The azaleas at Rikugi-en come into full blossom rather late in the season, usually at their best in late May to early June.

Construction of Rikugi-en, the Garden of the Six Principles of Poetry, began in the year 1695. The garden's name stands for the six principles used in the composition of Oriental poetry, and comes from the *Shi no Rikugi*, an anthology of Han Dynasty poems. Although you would have to be a scholar to identify them, the park's pond, flora and stones are said to embody 88 scenes described in the poetry form known as *waka*. The scenery, like many of these Edo era stroll gardens, was designed to evoke the spots described at 88 sites mentioned in major Chinese and Japanese literary works, in particular the settings found in two ancient Japanese poetry collections, the *Kokinwakashu* and the *Manyoshu*.

The building of this large, ambitiously conceived landscape took place under the supervision of Yanagisawa Yoshiyasu, a highly regarded art connoisseur, literati and horticulturist, who served as chamberlain to the Shogun Tokugawa Tsunayoshi. The garden took seven years to complete. After the death of Yanagisawa, the gardens became overgrown and untended. The neglect may have destroyed some of the original features of the landscape. The wealthy industrialist Iwasaki Yataro, founder of Mitsubishi, and something of a patron of

Right A view of the central pond from Fujimi-yama (Mount Fuji Viewing Peak), the 35 m summit of Fujishiro-toge, a hill named after a mountain pass in Wakayama prefecture. **Below** The view across the pond to Kamomeno-hashi, a short bridge connecting the main garden area to a large island.

venerable gardens, bought and restored the grounds in 1878.

Understanding the finer points of the design's literary or philosophical intentions is not a prerequisite for appreciating it. Most people are content to just enjoy the garden's curvaceous forms, the simple Zen-influenced design of its teahouses and the great profusion of trees, flowers and bushes that make the garden such a spiritually nourishing retreat. A shady place, with zelkova, dogwood, camphor and over 6,000 coniferous, evergreen and deciduous trees, the garden's 8.7 hectares are rarely crowded. A magnificent prospect of what is, arguably, the finest garden composition in Tokyo, is afforded from the summit of the artificial hill of Fujishiro-toge.

Above Reds, russets and yellows are the colors of autumn, a delightful season to stroll in the garden, particularly its border areas, which become rustling forest glades.

Top This section of the garden is a model of carefully designed ascending masses.

CHAPTER 4

requisitioning space

IDEALLY, SPACE SHOULD FLOW in much the same way as light—fluidly—following its own circulations. Water, the most sinuous of elements, a symbol of purity and the source of life, is a feature of almost every Japanese landscape design, even when it is only represented metaphorically. Its structure and flow determine the overall design, while its role as a mirror reflecting the sky, moon and stars adds to the depth and harmony of the garden.

Unity, proportion, balance, congruity and scale are as carefully considered in the garden composition as they are in traditional architecture. The convergence of gardens, architecture and environment suggests a symbiosis of spatial forms. Several creative methods are used to manage space in a garden, to ready visitors for a place of stillness and contemplation. Passing between tall, confining hedges, visitors may find themselves in a large open space; a zigzaging stone path increases the sense of distance between the

Opposite Space and repose at Kiyosumi-teien, a historical garden in the teeming downtown area of east Tokyo.

entrance and garden; a narrow gate creates a squeezed spatial context before visitors enter a garden whose proportions are in reality small, but now appear relatively ample. The dim light of the *genkan* or entrance, where visitors must remove their shoes before stepping onto *tatami* mats or polished planks for a more tactile experience of the garden architecture, slightly disorients one's trajectory, scrambling any preconceived spatial expectations.

Design principles combined with native instincts result in gardens epitomizing the Japanese sense of beauty and design, what one writer has termed the "overlapping of the rational and the random, the right angle and the natural form." In this respect, one of the dominant themes of Japanese architecture remains the interpenetration of inside and outside. The framing and rearrangement of space as a way of re-conceiving the garden and extending the interior into adjacent gardens is mediated by sliding *shoji* panels and paper *fusuma* doors. In its purest form, the reticulation of space requires that the created blends with creation, that inside and outside form a seamless whole.

The traditional house was constructed from timber, sedge and reed mats—natural materials requisitioned from the surrounding fields and forests. The garden was an extension of the dwelling. The interior of the house projected outwards. Its sliding doors revealed a panorama of nature enticed inwards. Its hanging scrolls and flower arrangements decorated the alcove of the main room. Symbiosis was favored over opposition.

Defining Space
... the gardener is held captive inside the garden and is unable to stop the flow of time. ... There is no completion for a garden. Time continues to flow forever.
—The architect Kuma Kengo

The subdivision of space makes gardens appear larger than their actual size, creating a sensation of boundlessness. When using rocks in the context of spatial manipulation, a gardener has two choices: to foreshorten space by using prominent stones in the distance and medium to small sized rocks in the middle ground, or to deepen the perspective by placing a massive rock in the foreground and smaller stones in the middle to distant planes, an effect that will promote a sense of depth. The three-dimensional aspect of a garden is often presented as two planes: the ground and elevational. The horizontal plane appears to be slightly tilted as it withdraws towards the distance. The visual illusion is adjusted, subtly fractured, by vertical rocks and trees, ponds and other physical elements within the garden.

Less obvious to the eye is the triangulation of forms and interlocking of planes within Japanese gardens. The ground and elevational planes are evident in two common rock groupings: Horizontal Triad Rocks (*hinbonseki*) and Buddhist Triad Rocks (*sanzonseki*). The triangle formed by the first grouping is flat, the second a more assertive vertical ensemble reminiscent of a central Buddhist deity flanked by two lesser divinities. The notion of a major form served

Left Water from a street culvert has been diverted beneath the walls of a private property, entering a small space that has converted the urban into the rural.

by two subordinate ones can form the design basis of entire gardens. The combination of both forms produces triangular masses that are at once static and kinetic. Stability and movement ground the garden to the site. If imaginary lines were composed between trees and rocks, the shapes to emerge would be scalene triangles, a fact that hints at the primacy of three-sided forms in the Japanese garden.

The Muromachi era aesthetic of *yugen*, an appreciation of the deeply austere and simple transfused with complex symbolism, and the use of empty, energizing space characterized by the expression *yohaku no bi*, are essential to stone garden design, but have wider applications among other Japanese landscape forms. The expanses of unarticulated space that characterize areas of the stone garden are only perceived as empty space in the most literal sense. More correctly, this is *ma*, a Japanese concept used in ink-wash landscape painting and music, where the dynamics of emptiness serve to

articulate space and form. Rather than being hollow or sterile, the void in landscape design emphasizes its existence by its absence, thereby adding to the determination of space and scale within the garden.

Visions of the Future

The making of a microcosm is not the same as miniaturization. Rather than reduce the cosmos, gardens attempt to expand their confines to proportions commensurate with the universe, if only metaphorically. Maximizing space, creating the illusion of a larger plot, is a practice that has applications for Western cities, where space is also at a premium. The Meiji era British architect, Josiah Conder, author of the first book on Japanese gardens in English, understood this when he wrote: "The Japanese garden reveals aesthetic principals applicable to the gardens of any country."

The preservation of gardens in their original form is determined to a large degree by environment. Provided that neither the garden nor its surroundings radically change, symbiosis can be maintained. This is almost impossible in the modern Japanese city where structures are allowed to grow virtually unchecked. The impact of environmental degradation on Japanese gardens is by no means a recent phenomenon. As Heian-kyo (present-day Kyoto) became more urbanized, the space and resources necessary for creating the kind of pond gardens favored by the aristocracy were restricted by water shortages. By the mid-twelfth century, deforestation of mountains and slopes close to the

city, and the consequent evaporation of ground water, had become sufficiently severe for the pond at the Higashi Sanjo Palace to have dried to a trickle.

Japanese gardens offer instructive models in space and environmental management, but respect for the laws that govern the natural world and sustain gardens have frequently gone unheeded. The Meiji period Rakuju-en garden in Mishima, for example, is an object lesson in the despoiling of nature. Several years ago the water in its pond suddenly vanished, exposing in the process a curious bed of irregular rock, the deposit from a lava flow some 12,000 years before, when Mount Fuji erupted. Partly due to a decrease in melting snow on the nearby volcano, the main cause for the draining was the construction of factories upriver and their overexploitation of water resources, resulting in the depletion of natural, replenishing aquifers. The sinking of wells for industrial usage has also lowered the water table in many other parts of the country.

Japanese cities can be a shock to the visual senses, with their wastelands of uncoordinated structures and poorly maintained surfaces. Streets, balefully devoid of greenery, disfigured by cobwebs of high-tension wires, often look unfinished. Visual distraction, overcrowding, noise and chemical pollution add to the sense of degradation. Where you might expect to find cities that embody a discreet prosperity, they speak of a poverty of taste. How can gardens survive in such traumatized environments?

If the challenge for gardens in the modern Japanese city is to restore a degree of serenity, the country's supremely resourceful landscape designers are better qualified than most to accomplish this. As the English architect Ralph Adams Cram observed in the Meiji era: "A Japanese gardener can work with anything—or almost nothing." Master gardeners possessed a highly developed understanding of space and microclimates, of how minute alterations in light, airflows, temperature and humidity levels could be adapted, skills contemporary landscape designers are requisitioning.

"Today, with the general loss of greenery, the trapping of heat in cities, and global warming," garden photographer Mizuno Katsuhiko has written, "the time has perhaps come for a second look at an urban life dependent on the supposed benefits of modern civilization." The ideal would be to create garden cities as opposed to cities with gardens. In space-depleted Japan, this remains in the realm of the theoretical, but the yearning for more proximate greenery, for gardens that can soften and moisten cityscapes that have become as hard and brittle as adamite, is intense.

Left In the contemporary garden, stone is often treated as a resource that can be cut and manipulated in much the same way as other structural or sculptural materials.

Opposite The abstractness of this dry landscape garden in Tokyo's Aoyama-ichome district is a surprisingly successful complement to the immediate cityscape.

Kyu Shiba-Rikyu Onshi Garden

旧芝離宮恩賜庭園

This easily overlooked landscape, also known as the Shiba Detached Palace, is a scrupulously designed Edo period stroll garden located near to Tokyo Bay. Floating at the center of the garden's large pond are five islands. The largest, Horai-jima, a rocky island covered in black pine, takes its name from Taoist mythology, which tells of five islands to the east of China where the Immortals lived in perfect harmony. Pines were venerated in China as symbols of immortality, and Taoist teachings encouraged monks to eat the cones, resin and needles in order to acquire the life force of the tree.

An example of resourceful reclamation, marshland in the area was drained and filled to make the landscape. A typical *daimyo* garden, and one of the oldest formal landscapes in the city, construction began in 1678. A relatively small garden of only 4.3 hectares, what it lacks in scale it more than makes up for in conception, particularly apparent in the sensitive layout around the central pond.

Type **Stroll garden**
Designer **Gardeners from the Odawara domain**
Period **Late 17th century**
Location **Kaigan, Minato-ku, Tokyo**

Other features of the garden worth noting are its carefully laid out clusters of rocks, a *karetaki ishigumi* (dry waterfall rock arrangement), groves of zelkova and chinquapin, a wisteria trellis and various artificial hills and mounds. The tallest, called Nebukawa Yama, has 26 stone steps leading to its summit.

Much reduced in size over the centuries, the fate of the garden in the

Above The Chinese influence is evident in this bridge, a replica of the causeway transecting the West Lake in Hangzhou.
Opposite The garden's distinctive three-legged, snow viewing lantern.

modern age is to have found itself surrounded by rail tracks, high-rise offices, expressways and elevated monorails. Despite that, it somehow manages to seem like a retreat. Sea breezes pass across the garden, which is the sometime home of black-headed gulls, a reminder of how close it once stood to the bay and the views that were to be had before development encroached on the area. The garden was designated an important scenic spot in 1979 and is unlikely, natural disasters notwithstanding, to be further altered.

Above Several hillocks help to add contouring and undulation to the garden.

Opposite far left Modern encroachments on what was once an area of tidal flats.

Opposite above Irises, strongly associated with the rainy season in Japan, are a common seasonal signal in gardens.

Opposite below A native of Japan and northern China, various strains of iris became important horticultural plants in gardens in the early part of the Edo era.

Left This single azalea bush appears to be an afterthought to the original garden, but adds a dash of color in late spring.

Above Flat granite bridges are a common feature of Japanese gardens, serving as transitions between contrasting sections.

Koishikawa Koraku-en

小石川後楽園

Type **Stroll garden**
Period **Early 17th century**
Commissioned by **Tokugawa Yorifusa**
Location **Iidabashi, Bunkyo-ku, Tokyo**

Laid out in 1629, Koshikawa Korakuen is Tokyo's oldest garden. Edo period gardens were greatly influenced by Chinese landscaping styles. Within the garden, many famous spots in China and Japan have been re-created in miniature for the enjoyment and edification of visitors.

The garden was constructed under the orders of Tokugawa Yorifusa, founder of the Mito clan, a branch of the powerful Tokugawa family. The work was completed by the head of the second generation of the family, Mitsukuni, a great patron of learning. The name Korakuen (A Place to Take Pleasure After) is derived from a Chinese poem by Fan Zhongyan, which reads: "Be the first to take the world's trouble to heart, be the last to enjoy the world's pleasures." Tempering those pleasures, a rice field in one section of the garden was placed there with the intention of teaching his heir's wife the hardships of farming.

Left Each season has its own colors. In spring, cherry blossoms cascade into the waters of a large pond called Osensui.
Right A pond of sacred lotus beneath a bamboo grass hill depicting Mount Lu in China's Jiangxi Province.

A stroll garden with a large central pond, its grounds were designed by Tokudaiji Sahei with the assistance of Zhu Shunsui, a Confucian scholar and refugee from the fall of the Ming Dynasty. Mitsukuni took great note of the opinions of Shunsui, who is said to have designed the Engetsukyo Bridge, an exquisite "full moon" span in the Chinese style. Though largely ornamental, it may very well be the oldest intact bridge in the city. Another Chinese reference can be found in an earthen watercourse running through the center of the garden's small river, a reproduction of a dike that passes through Hangzhou Bay in China. A small hill near the pond represents Mount Lu in Jiangxi Province. The slopes of the mound are covered in bamboo grass, while at its base is a pond of sacred lotus.

The original Koishikawa Korakuen extended to 28 hectares. The present garden covers a much reduced, but manageable seven hectares. In pre-Edo days, the site was the location of a shallow lake, an arm of Tokyo Bay. With its large pond, islets, winding paths, plum orchard, iris garden, stone lanterns and teahouses, this is a wonderful introduction to Japanese gardens in general, and to the stroll garden in particular.

The downside of the garden's location is its proximity to the Tokyo Dome and the Korakuen Amusement Park roller coaster. However, the garden itself was originally designed and laid out as a kind of theme park, a recreational space for the Mito clan to entertain privileged visitors, clamber up its miniature hills, stage poetry parties and float in barges on its pond.

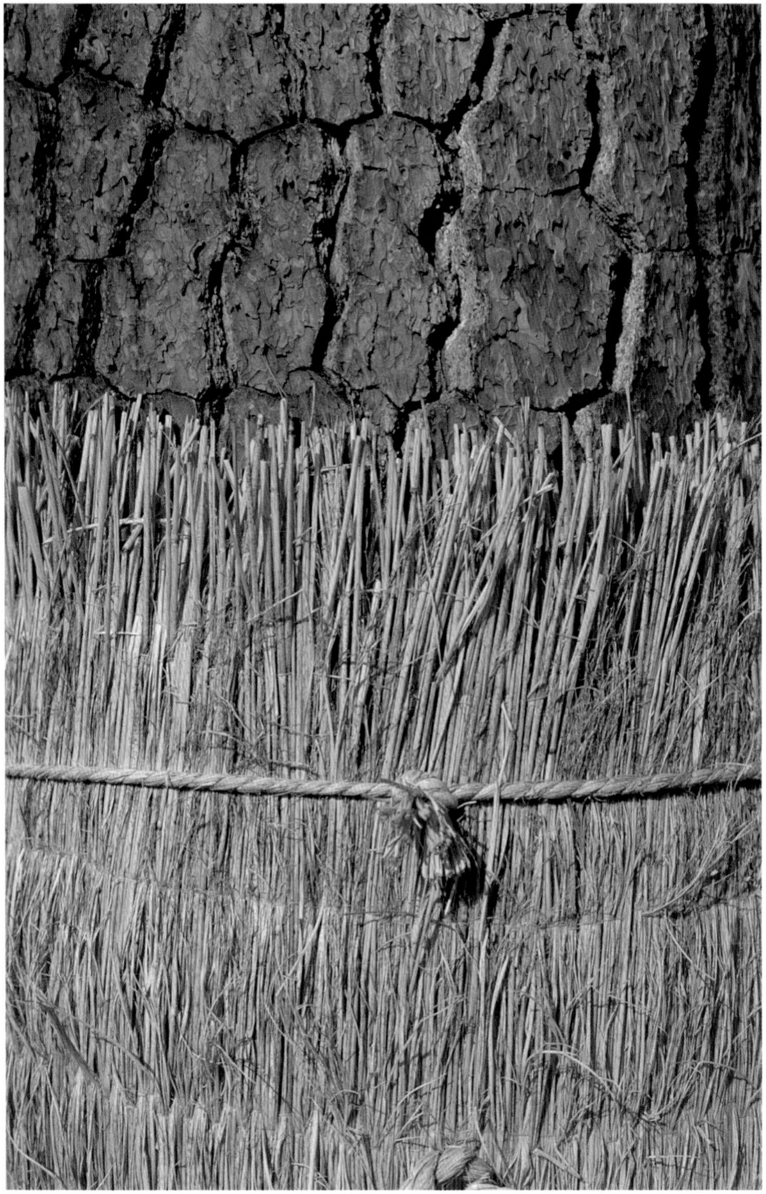

Left Straw trusses are placed around some of the more temperature sensitive trees during the winter. In the spring, the material, whose warmth attracts insects, is removed.
Opposite above Lily pads cover the surface of the pond in the Nantei or Inner Garden where the Mito clan once maintained a *shoin*-style guesthouse.
Opposite below A large water laver placed for mostly decorative purposes near the lotus pond.

Below from left to right Vines resting during the winter months on a wisteria trellis in the northern section of the garden. Cherry blossoms floating in the marshy field where irises are cultivated. Rectangular stones reinforce a section of an embankment.
Bottom A miniaturized reproduction of the dike that runs across Hangzhou Bay in China crosses the Oigawa River in the western portion of the garden.

In Japan, stroll gardens are synonymous with grand estates and castles. Built beside a detached palace at the base of Hikone Castle on the orders of Ii Nao-oki in 1677, Genkyu-en, a two hectare circulation garden with an outstanding borrowed view of the castle floating above a thickly wooded slope, is a digest of various style canons.

Named after the Tang period detached palace of the Chinese emperor Xuan Song, its bold rock groupings are reminders of the assertive *samurai* aesthetics of the Momoyama period (1568–1600), while its large pond, replete with four islands based on the Isles of the Immortals in Chinese mythology, speak of the design tastes of the early Edo era.

Throughout, rocks have been carefully implanted into the landscape. One particular set replicates the Eight Views of the Omi region; others represent the white rocks of Oki, and an island known as Chichibu-jima. If the rock settings at Genkyu-en represent the martial leanings of the domain lords of the time, the garden's pavilions and teahouses, cantilevered above the edges of the pond and offering superb views across the water, speak of a connoisseurship in Japanese aesthetics and the conduct of the tea ceremony.

Genkyu-en

玄宮園

Type **Stroll garden**
Period **Late 17th century**
Commissioned by **Ii Nao-oki**
Location **Hikone, Shiga prefecture**

Top A skillfully placed stone lantern adds interest to the edges of the pond.
Opposite A captured view of Hikone Castle, which has changed little since the garden's creation.

Right Carefully positioned master rocks link water expanses to the garden's built structures.
Below The bold, assertive rocks of a dry landscape garden placed within the grounds of the Raku-raku-en Palace, a recently renovated structure within the garden.

The Hosodai teahouse, with its red carpets, period lampshades and contemplative atmosphere, is named to express the sense of a commanding height, where the Chinese phoenix soars to the sky. The structure was listed as one of the garden's major scenic spots in the painting "Genyu-en zu," completed in the Edo period. Lavishly painted boats, with feudal lords and their guests sailing on the pond, appear in the work.

Part of the charm of the garden is that it is not overly maintained; tufts of grass grow on banks and last autumn's dry leaves nestle in the root cradles of trees. The garden's terraced and thatched buildings also have a mildly ramshackle appearance, but inside a quiet elegance asserts itself.

Right A classic wooden trestle bridge.
Below left Garden teahouses in Japan often afford the best views. The Hosoda teahouse is no exception.
Below right A thatched roof teahouse overgrown with moss, a naturalistic effect typical of a garden that is not overly maintained.

Canadian Embassy Garden

カナダ大使館庭園

Type **Dry landscape garden**
Period **1991**
Designer **Shunmyo Masuno**
Location **Canadian Embassy, Aoyama-ichome, Tokyo**

Improbably sited in front of the fourth floor reception of the embassy, many of the rocks used in the garden were cut to size and then hollowed out, a contentious but necessary measure given their problematic weight.

Using rocks transported from Hiroshima, this 1991 masterwork represents the geological character of the rocks that form the Canadian Shield, while highlighting the ideal of harmony through the friendship between Japan and Canada.

The Japanese stone garden is singularly well suited to the urban setting, the interminable expanses of glass and concrete recalling the bleakness of mountain ranges depleted of plants and greenery. Pollution and limited sunshine often conspire against growing healthy plants in urban areas, a problem that designers of stone gardens are not obliged to consider.

Opposite This section of the garden, requisitioning a dense tree line and combining sky, water and solid matter, seems to float above the city.

Below Flagstones intersect with cut stones and more naturalistic slabs of rock and loose gravel.

While it has been suggested in the modern context that the dry surfaces of skyscrapers and apartment blocks can usefully serve as borrowed scenery for the contemporary garden, the elevated terrace of the embassy benefits from being able to requisition some natural features in the form of the seasonally changing foliage of the spacious grounds of the Akasaka Palace on one side, and the trees of an adjoining park, the Takahashi Memorial Gardens, on the other.

The designer, Shunmyo Masuno, the head priest of a Zen temple in Yokohama, is singularly well qualified to create meaningful gardens in the contemporary context. Shunmyo has said: "To make a good garden, the first thing one must do is to let one's spirit mature. In this sense, landscape gardening is spiritual training."

Standing on a narrow, granite projectory above a sheet of water at the edge of the embassy shelf, with the upper tree line of Akasaka Palace serving as a cleanly framed horizontal panel, the visitor feels an integral part of both the city and a highly sculptured landscape.

Right Shunmyo Masuno's iconic stone garden, a homage to the Canadian landscape, is a surprisingly apt visual complement to the high rises of Tokyo.

Below left A checker-board of stone and gravel, similar to a traditional *ichimatsu* design, resembles a mountainside view of rice fields.

Below right The random, fragmented appearance of these rocks replicates geological plates.

Left Because of their weight, many of the larger slabs of rock that sit on the upper, exposed terrace of the embassy, have been hollowed out to make them lighter.

Above Some sections of the dry landscape seem closer to sculpture than garden design.

The disposition and use of space in Tokyo, a city once renowned for its greenery and open public areas, has become a pressing issue. Gardens that have kept their spatial integrity in the face of urban encroachment are something of a miracle in the world's largest megacity.

Built within the grounds of a former estate in an area close to the Sumida River, the Kiyosumi-teien garden is a surprisingly refined creation to stumble across in this otherwise densely populated district of east Tokyo. Like other historic gardens in Tokyo, it has an interesting history of ownership and change. Part of a larger estate belonging to the wealthy seventeenth-century timber merchant Kinokuniya Bunzaemon, the garden fell on hard times. After further ownership exchanges, the land was bought up in 1878 by Iwasaki Yatoro, founder of the Mitsubishi industrial group. Painstaking renovation of the original garden was completed by 1885.

Iwasaki's brother, Yanosuke, an art connoisseur, spent a great deal of time and money selecting rare and lovely rocks from all over Japan, which were then transported to Tokyo in the company's steamships. The original garden was designed around water, a template that remains intact.

Kiyosumi-teien

清澄庭園

Type **Stroll garden**
Period **Late 19th century**
Commissioned by **Kinokuniya Bunzaemon**
Restoration **Iwasaki Yatoro**
Location **Kiyosumi, Koto-ku, Tokyo**

Top An impressive *isowatari* or stepping-stone path close to the garden entrance.
Opposite A rare snowfall turns the garden into a silent winter world.

Left A good deal of thought has gone into the placement of rocks against the garden's embankments.
Below Azaleas and green, grass-like *tama-ryu* ("dragon balls") soften the effect of dark rocks.

Right A bamboo pipe conducts water in a stone laver, creating a refreshing soundtrack during the humid summer months.

The grounds, which now occupy an area of 3.8 hectares, are surrounded by tall, mature trees, creating a sense of privacy and seclusion. Bird lovers will appreciate the waterfowl that collect here, from wintering ducks to all-year azure-winged magpies. Gazebos, a carp-filled pond, a miniature Mount Fuji and other landscape trappings lend interest to this quiet, generously proportioned garden. A central feature of the design is a traditional Japanese teahouse constructed in 1909 to host Lord Kitchener on his official state visit from England.

Kiyosumi-teien is an all-seasons garden. In spring, forsythia, cherry, Japanese andromeda, quince and azaleas are at their best. Summer sees the blooming of irises, gardenia, hydrangea, crepe myrtle and Japanese catalpa. During the autumn months, fragrant olive, camellia and red spider come into their own, while winter is the time for plum, wandflower and pheasant's eye.

In these colder months, rice-straw mats are wrapped around the pine trunks. The mats, which attract heat-seeking insects, are removed and then burnt in the spring. At this time, the garden's pine trees are strung with supports called *yuki-tsuri*, whose ropes form a cone shape. These prevent heavy snowfall from breaking the branches. With climate change, a phenomena as potentially transforming as urbanization, the function of the rope frames is becoming more and more decorative as the snows that once spoke of deep winter stay away from the city.

Left The Ryotei, a teahouse built as a guesthouse for the visit of Lord Kitchener in 1909. The rocks in the foreground were brought by steamship from different regions of Japan after being carefully selected by Iwasaki Yanosuke, an art connoisseur.

Above A view of Tsurushima, a small island, from the arbor on another islet called Naka-no-shima.

CHAPTER 5

healing gardens

IT IS SAID THAT ONE of the best ways to become a person of culture and taste is the study of the Japanese tea ceremony, where nothing is permitted to be rushed and where there are no short cuts to accomplishment. In the contemporary age, the finer sensibilities risk being blunted and coarsened. The number of aesthetically attuned guests at a tea ceremony gathering who listen in rapture to the sound of iron filings at the bottom of the *cha-gama* (teapot) because it reminds them of the sound of wind souring through pine trees, are few and far between. The gardens of our own age are able, however, if only for a brief moment, to restore an appreciation of detail, to reconnect us to nature, to decelerate the process of time.

tea flowers—
their blooming
delays the dusk
—The Buddhist nun Chiyo-ni

Left The east garden of Nara's Isui-en, with its distant captured view.

Gardens are as much a part of our lives as the currents and forces of nature. To meet someone who openly professes to dislike gardens is as rare as the person who declares a distaste for music. To deny ourselves contact with gardens is somehow counter-intuitive. A Chinese proverb has it that "Life begins on the day you start a garden." The pleasures of life in the ancient Chinese garden are well recorded. The Qing scholar Chen Fuyao, writing in the *Huajing* (Flower Mirror) in 1688, recalls winter as a time for munching on charcoal-baked yams, sipping tea brewed from cracked ice taken from gardens or field, of "watching the slow-moving tree shadows on garden steps, and enjoying washing my feet in hot water." Like the Chinese, the Japanese believed in the benefits of living in a harmonious and well-balanced environment, one that promoted health, well-being, even longevity. The master gardens of Japan are still places to sit quietly with a book of classic poems, or to contemplate landscapes of stone and water while sipping from a bowl of fragrant, powdered green tea.

Reprising Nature

Since the Dewy Path
Is a way that lies outside
This most impure world

Shall we not
Cleanse our hearts on entering it
From earthly mire?
—Sen-no-Rikyu

There is no place for anxiety or neurosis in the garden. Once entered, if only for a short space of time, we are able to slough off the real and metaphorical grime of our everyday lives. We return from the experience reinvigorated, spiritually cleansed. In his widely read *Zazen wasan* (The Song of Meditation), the monk Hakuin wrote:

Open the vastness of unobstructed repose,
Bask in the brilliance of complete wisdom.

What better place to experience "unobstructed repose" than in the Japanese garden? As we enter the garden we experience a stalling of time, a deepening of the senses, a stilling of the negative emotions that cause stress.

Where we may recoil from the immensity of the wilderness, we embrace gardens which, being created by man, mirror our own sensibilities. It is possible to see in the design of a garden the thoughts of its creator or the person who commissioned it.

It had not been a garden of hidden meanings.
But now her new perception of the garden
opened up new levels of feeling, and she
began to re-examine her emotions.
— Tachihara Masaki, *Wind and Stone*

Blending spirit and matter, our affinity with gardens is as much genetic as cultural, rooted perhaps in our evolution amidst a fertile world of forests and green plains.

Opposite Early blooming irises in a marshy patch of the Nezu Museum Garden.

In periods of savage warfare and civic turmoil, temples and gardens served as both places of physical refuge and spiritual solace. Scholar, hermitage and literary gardens have long been cherished as retreats, but in the modern world, where prolonged introspection is not always possible, gardens perform the function of sanctuaries from which we can return to our normal lives restored and re-energized.

Engrossed in ourselves for much of the time, when we enter a garden it forces us outwards into a fresh consideration of nature. No one will emerge from a garden transformed, but the exposure can have beneficial effects that are not immediately apparent but nonetheless perform a quiet alchemy on our thinking, the way we feel about the world.

The flow of organic time within the garden is quite different from the movement of social time that we are usually subject to. In decelerating time, gardens still the nerves, engage the mind and, in some instances, even reduce the pulse rate. Spending time in gardens may seem like escapism, but a better word might be connection. The sound of a waterfall, bringing to mind a natural setting of serenely quiet mountains, is a sensation that can be reintroduced back into our lives. Gardens counterbalance the negativity experienced outside its enclosures. By introducing selected elements in nature into the garden, the landscape designer creates a setting for intellectual calm and psychological repose. The garden induces a dual but compatible response—making us relaxed but mindful, calm but fully aware, serene but alert.

The traditional Japanese gardener does not think of himself as an outsider, but as an element in the landscape, part of the spirit of the garden itself. If we carry the spirit of the garden within us, we can face material reality with a greater degree of composure and equanimity. Traditionally, a husband returning from work would repair first to the room overlooking a modest garden, where he would sit and gaze at the space before him for a short period before joining his family. Although the custom has for the most part fallen from practice, this process of rebalancing is one that we can learn from.

A detailed understanding of design principles, the occult cosmology that underlies many of the more ancient gardens, is not required to feel a sense of liberation and release at stepping into a Japanese garden. Unraveling the mysteries and concealed meanings of designs can be immensely rewarding, but overstraining to conceptualize or interpret Japanese gardens can be a peculiarly counter-productive endeavor, one that can diminish their intended effect, the natural exhilaration felt in first glimpsing them. On more than one occasion I have seen very young children, led into gardens by their nervous minders, let out a whoop of joy, discovering in the expanse of hills, shingle, water and rock set out before them a timeless cosmos, an infinity of nothing less than sheer pleasure.

Serenity Now

The scholar-gardeners of China believed in creating metaphorical parallels between natural forms and human emotions, holding, for example, that summer mountains covered in shady forests induced calm and poise; that wisps of misty cloud threading across mountain landscapes engendered alertness and contentment. These images were incorporated into garden designs with the intention of stimulating emotions and bringing about atmospheric changes in mood.

The ancient city of Kyoto, a place of multiple moods and quintessential Japanese culture, opens many of its iconic, much-photographed gardens to the public. An alternative side to the city is its residential gardens. These private spaces exert a benevolent influence, though in a discreet, silent manner, as Zen authority Suzuki T. Daisetz noted when he wrote: "The existence of these invisible gardens lends the city a stillness, an indescribable depth."

Gardens exert powers that cast us into a state of suspended thrall by creating a world that is profound, unsullied and luminous. The water in a stone basin reflects the sky, imbuing a sense of purity into the garden. Burning a green mosquito coil in the garden produces an ancient smell, somewhere between incense and grass, temple and wilderness. There is nothing quite like sitting on a shaded wooden verandah, or sipping a bowl of slightly astringent powdered green tea, pausing to listen to the cries of summer cicadas while breathing in the acrid scents, a stillness that is faintly tranquilizing. These are the textures and sensations of a Japanese garden.

Quiet, uncluttered, reposeful, gardens satisfy a longing for plentiude, contact with nature and the poetic, spiritual fulfillment. Gardens that incorporate religious and philosophical ideas or embody a vision of paradise are idealized landscapes hinting at the way the world might be. Because many of the elements in the garden are taken from the actual world, the implication is that paradise already exists in our own realm of being, though we may not always be aware of it. Gardens illuminate the wonders of the world we live in.

In this natural but refined milieu, Japanese master gardens represent not merely a model for the metamorphosis of nature into art, aesthetic pleasure and philosophical profundity, but a place for self-cultivation and healing. We would be wise to take a little time to stop and listen to nature in its most representational and abstract garden forms, for what it has to say is invariably worth listening to.

Below Circular stones form a *isowatari* or stepping-stone path across a still pond. **Opposite** This plate from the Edo era gardening manual, *Tsukiyama Teizoden* (Building Mountains and Making Gardens), has as its focal point a snow viewing stone lantern.

Mukojima Hyakka-en

向島百花園

Type **Literary garden**
Period **Early 19th century**
Commissioned by **Sahara Kiku**
Location **Higashi Mukojima, Sumida-ku, Tokyo**

Above A bamboo stand carved in stone reinforces the idea of the garden as a horticultural center.

Opposite The garden's celebrated *hagi* (bush clover) tunnel is bare in the spring and summer months, the flowers coming into bloom in September.

In the spring, wisteria,
rippling like waves,
blooming like a holy purple cloud,
also to the west.
—Hojoki, *Kamo-no-Chomei*

By the late years of Meiji, an exquisite culture of taste, embodied in the teahouses and cherry trees that lined the embankments of the Sumida River at Mukojima in Tokyo, was still possible to sense, despite the appearance of smokestacks and the spillage from coal barges.

Although it remains one of the capital's least visited Edo period gardens, the name Mukojima Hyakka-en is widely known. Built around 1805, the garden, close in spirit to the literary landscapes of Chinese and Korean scholars, covers little more than a hectare, but is intensely planted with trees, deciduous shrubs,

Left Much of the garden, including its water channels, was damaged during the air raids of World War II, but the grounds were faithfully restored to their present state in 1949.
Opposite below Large numbers of visitors come to this otherwise tranquil garden in the month of September to view its famous tunnel of *hagi* (bush clover).

flowering bushes and herbaceous perennials.

Sahara Kiku, a wealthy antique dealer in the Nihonbashi district, had the garden built in a style that was a rejoinder to the overelaborate landscapes created for the city's military elite and aristocratic class. The absence of great stones, rocks and reproductions in miniature of famous scenes is rare for this period of thematic gardens. Instead, the name Hyakka-en means "The Garden of One Hundred Flowers," a reference to the selection of flowers and plants here, all with connections to the arts and literature. Many of Sahara's writer and artist friends lent a hand inscribing stones with poems, quotations and aphorisms. The inclusion of seasonal herbs, bottle and snake gourds, bush clover and wild pampas lend the garden a naturalistic character.

Donated to the city by Sahara's descendants in 1938, the garden was severely damaged during the air raids of World War II. After the war, it was carefully restored to its present condition. The garden's literary and aesthetic traditions live on in full moon viewing events, insect listening appreciation in the summer months, and the gathering on spring and autumn evenings of *haiku* poets.

Above from left to right
The *basho*, a type of banana tree, adds an exotic touch to the garden, but is also a reference to the great *haiku* poet Matsuo Basho, who took his literary name from the plant. A trellis growing the curious *hebi-uri* or snake gourd. Spring azaleas add a touch of color to a garden mostly composed of wild plants, herbs and grasses. Designed as an open-air literary salon, there are 89 stone engravings of poems in the garden, 14 of which are *haiku*.

Zuisen-ji Garden

瑞泉寺

Type **Dry landscape garden**
Period **Early 14th century**
Designer **Muso Soseki**
Temple complex **Zuisen-ji**
Location **Momijigayatsu, northeast Kamakura**

Fading temple bell
The fragrance of flowers strikes
At evening
—Basho

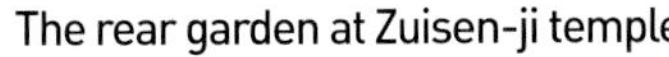

The rear garden at Zuisen-ji temple is located in the green northeastern belt of Kamakura. The temple was founded in 1327 by an extraordinary man, the Buddhist prelate Muso Soseki, an astonishingly gifted Zen master and garden designer.

The grounds are approached via steep stone steps that rise beneath dark cryptomerias and bamboo glades that are cool even in summer, partly because of the tree overhang, but also the dark earth that holds its moisture, a feature of these cliff-abutting north-eastern temple grounds.

Zuisen-ji consists of an intensely planted front garden, with a formal schematic of stone paths geometrically aligned with the temple buildings. Despite the grid, the garden appears to be highly naturalistic, with crops of plum, cherry, hydrangeas, narcissus, peonies and Chinese bellflower

Left Visitors must pass through the garden to reach the main hall of the temple.
Right Muso Soseki co-opted a section of the rocky bluff at the rear of the temple and, with only the slightest of adjustments, converted it into a dry landscape garden.

complementing the dark, stained wood of the temple.

The stone garden at the rear is only slightly arranged, the cave and pond being natural features, but the design, bare, stripped of flowers, plants or stone additions, can be ranked a masterpiece of Zen austerity. A quarried alcove and inner shelving suggest the former presence of Buddhist statuary. The effect of this dry landscape is, perhaps, more naturalistic than beautiful, the cliffs and caves suggesting less a garden in the formal sense than something akin to the sacred Buddha caves at Tuqoq in the far desert reaches of Western China, or the gardens of old Korean rural residences, where a forest or cliff is co-opted as the garden itself.

Whether Soseki's experiment with the dry landscape garden resonates with the early pre-Shinto proto-gardens found in forest glades, or the rock arrangements, early stone gardens made in ancient times on the edges of Chinese deserts, rather depends on the visitors' gifts of re-imagination. The two very distinct gardens at Zuisen-ji are sometimes interpreted as the dual sides of reality, the designs apparently in opposition but actually in perfect harmony.

Top This small but intricate garden includes a number of short flower walks.
Above Flowers growing in natural profusion provide ground cover for a scene that resembles a bosky wood.

Opposite far left Zuisen-ji can get busy when a particular tree or flower is in bloom, but otherwise remains a still sanctuary.

Right The rear of the temple in early autumn. Later in the season, the entire hill will turn into a brocade of red, gold and orange leaf.

Below Though carefully arranged, pockets of the garden look completely naturalistic.

Nezu Museum Garden

根津美術館庭園

Type **Generic circulation garden**
Period **Mid-20th century**
Commissioned by **Nezu Kaichiro**
Location **Minami-Aoyama, Tokyo**

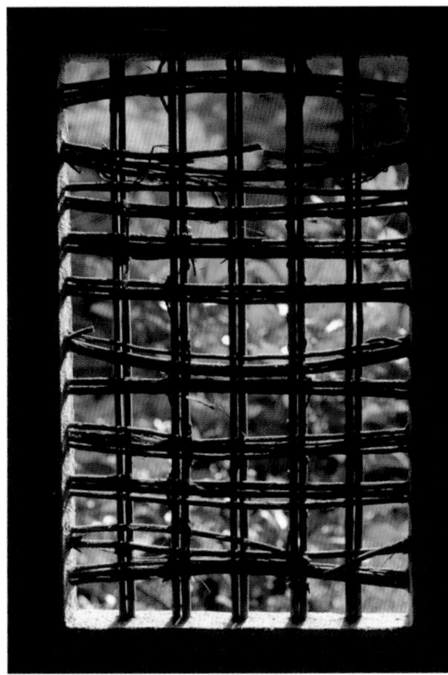

This museum of fine art and its equally exquisite garden opened to the public in 1941, the year after the death of its founder, the Taisho era railway giant Nezu Kaichiro. The garden is a wonderful hybrid of Japanese, Chinese and Western circulation patterns. It was really only men of culture and wealth who could afford to indulge their taste in the kind of stylistic integration evident here.

Kuma Kengo, designer of the current museum, completed in 2009, has said: "I treated the museum as a gate connecting the city and the sacred garden." The structure also acts as a filter, muting the sound from the busy Omotesando district, replacing an urban soundtrack with bird song, the rustle of last autumn's leaves and the hum of summer insects.

In the garden, built on a hillside planted with bamboo and maples, visitors pass rustic teahouses before reaching a long, narrow pond. The garden is not ancient in the historical

Left An autumn scene viewed through the window of a traditional teahouse.
Right A light well forms between trees in a section of the pond, providing the perfect space for a patch of early irises.

sense, but an atmosphere of antiquity pervades it. As you follow its paths, dense foliage envelopes a number of authentic stone and bronze artifacts, religious iconography, seated Buddhas, steles, a bronze temple bell and stone lanterns. There are more visual surprises in the form of a rotting, half-sunken barge, weighed down by water and moss, a bronze elephant god statue with a two-story pagoda on its back, a Ming Dynasty stone stele with a carved Buddha from China, a 13-story stone pagoda and a Muromachi period Ksitigarbhas carved stone triad.

There is no single route in or out of the garden, encouraging a sensation of serendipity and freedom. Covering five acres of intense woodland and water, this discreetly concealed, intensely green sanctuary, a cross between a natural site and a tea garden, offers a spiritual alternative to the materialism of the city.

Above from left to right A spray of lilies, a rare sight in this garden. This Buddhist statue appears to have appealed to the generosity of passersby. A stone pagoda adds interest to the garden's rich mix of ornamentation.
Right May is the best time to catch the simultaneous flowering of azaleas and irises.

Opposite above left Moss grows well in this shady, slightly humid climate.
Opposite below left A dusting of moss covers many of the Buddhist statues collected by Nezu Kaichiro.
Opposite right Autumn leaves have been allowed to gather on the roof of this teahouse in order to stress the rustic character of the garden.

Isui-en

依水園

Type **Stroll and pond garden**
Period **Late 17th century; late 19th century**
Designer **Seki Tojiro (east garden)**
Location **Nara**

Top Stepping-stones once used for grinding dye pigments cross the east garden pond.
Left The sublime Sanshu-tei tea ceremony house dates from the mid-Edo period.

Lotus flowers
three of them opened and
the pond narrows
—Shiki

Isui-en consists of two interconnected gardens. Access to the east garden from the older western section of the grounds is via stepping-stones passing between the Seishun and Tei-shu-ken teahouses, modest structures of the understated rustic beauty typical of an older tea ceremony aesthetic.

The more intimate west garden was created in the Enpo era (1673–1681) by a rich Nara bleacher and ramie textile maker named Kiyosumi Michikiyo. He modified the original layout and erected two houses, the Sanshu-tei and Tei-shu-Ken, as the family villa, to which artists, literati and admirers of the tea ceremony were invited.

The larger rear garden to the east was designed by Seki Tojiro in 1899. The stepping-stones leading across the pond to a small island were once used as mortars in the process of sizing ramie cloth, an interesting reference to Kiyosumi's trade.

The main pond in front of the Hyoshin-tei is dug in the shape of the Chinese character for *mizu* (water). This is a refreshing alternative to

Left A view across the east garden pond towards a collection of teahouses.
Below The garden's white lotuses come into full bloom in the high summer months of July and August.

the garden convention of creating *shinji no ike* ponds in a configuration deriving from the ideogram for "heart." Surrounded with miniature trees and carefully trimmed bushes, white lotuses bloom at the edges of the pond.

Hyoshin-tei is the best spot from which to appreciate the garden's borrowed view, which incorporates the tiled roof of Nandaimon, the Great Southern Gate of Todai-ji temple, and part of the huge roof of its Great Buddha Hall, elements adding divinity to nature. The layered view integrates lush hillside plantings, a row of tree-tops near Himuro Shrine, and the more distant outlines of Mount Kasugaoku, Wakakusa and Mikasa.

Artificial slopes and banks of azalea bulk up in a rising vista typical of the Meiji era, when flowering bushes were used as substitutes for rocks in providing mass and contouring. The original perspective remains unblemished by modern buildings or high-tension lines. Garden historian Gunter Nitschke has called it "perhaps the most outstanding example of *shakkei* in the entire Meiji era." The framing, though, is not without its detractors. Garden writer Itoh Teiji has noted: "If there is any fault in the view, it is that the line of the hill Wakakusayama cuts across the roof lines of the gate and thus produces a certain instability in the composition."

Below The view of the west garden's small pond from the verandah of the Sanshu-tei tea ceremony house.

Right The exquisite Sanshu-tei tea house is reached by crossing a stone bridge across a pond filled with crane and turtle islands. Auspicious seashells are embedded in the roofs of the teahouse.

Shikina-en

識名園

Type **Stroll garden**
Period **Late 18th century**
Commissioned by **Ryukyu royal family**
Location **Naha, Okinawa**

Okinawan garden design and horticulture reflect not only climatic differences but disparities in taste and cultural preferences from mainland Japan. Serving as a large second residence for the Ryukyu royal family, construction of Naha's Shikina-en, also known as the Shichina-Nu-Udun, was completed in 1799. Udun Palace, a set of wooden buildings and terraces with red-tiled roofs, stands near the entrance to the garden. Serving as a detached villa, Chinese delegates would gather in its fifteen rooms for the coronation of Ryukyu royalty.

The garden was painstakingly reconstructed over a twenty-year period after the site was obliterated in World War II. Looking at prewar photos of the garden, the current restoration is an astonishingly faithful one, right down to the wooden buildings and pavilions. In 2000, the garden was registered as a UNESCO World Heritage site.

Banana groves remind the visitor that they are firmly in the subtropics. Continental Asia asserts itself in the Rokkaku-do, a small Chinese-style pavilion of hexagonal design. Such was the refinement of older Chinese gardens that waterfront pavilions were built to admire the sound of the rain, kiosks erected solely for the purpose

Above The modest but graceful buildings of the Sho kings glimpsed from the Rokkaku-do.
Opposite A causeway resembling the flat bridge that crosses the dike running through the western section of Hangzhou Bay in China.

Left The Chinese-style bridge and Okinawan royal pavilions create a mood that is very different from that found in the gardens of mainland Japan.

of listening to the wind. Constructed as a space to rest and admire the circular views of the garden, the arched bridge leading to the Rokkaku-do is carved from a single piece of Ryukyu limestone.

Limestone compositions in the classic Chinese garden consisted of fabulist piles of energizing rocks full of blowholes, scooped surfaces, cavities and hollows, a playful effect still much beloved of the Chinese and a characteristic of Shikina-en. The Chinese influence, however important, should not be emphasized at the expense of native Okinawan instincts. Although there was symbolism embedded in the gardens of Okinawan royalty, the adoption of Chinese forms was mostly visual and aesthetic. Complex notions like the belief among Taoist scholars that a private garden was an articulation of a yearning for a graceful, happy, long life in retirement had little place in the exuberant flower- and plant-filled gardens of these islanders.

Steering clear of the demanding symbolism of the Japanese garden, most visitors to both Japanese and Okinawan landscapes would feel perfectly comfortable with the simple sentiments of the Ming era Chinese writer and gardener Wen Zhenheng when he wrote that gardens are places where the visitor should be able to "forget their age, forget to go home, and forget their fatigue."

Above The superbly sited Rokkaku-do, the garden's Chinese-style hexagonal pavilion.
Right This Chinese-influenced limestone bridge is a fine example of the kind of pitted, fabulist rock favored by Okinawans.
Opposite below The generously proportioned pond at Shikina-en provides a constant change of angle and perspective on the garden.

Bibliography

Cali, Joseph, *The New Zen Garden: Designing Quiet Spaces*, Kodansha International, Tokyo, 2004.

Carver, Norma, *Form and Space in Japanese Architecture and Gardens*, Documan, Kalamazoo, Maryland, 1991.

Cho Wang, Joseph, *The Chinese Garden*, Oxford University Press, Hong Kong, 1998.

Conder, Josiah, *Landscape Gardening in Japan*, Kodansha International, Tokyo, 2002 [1893].

Earle, Joe (ed.), *Infinite Spaces: The Art and Wisdom of the Japanese Garden*, Tuttle Publishing, Tokyo, 2000.

Einarsen, John, *Zen and Kyoto*, Uniplan, Kyoto, 2004.

Harte, Sunniva, *Zen Gardening*, Pavilion Books, London, 1999.

Holborn, Mark, *The Ocean in the Sand: Japan: From Landscape to Garden*, Gordon Fraser, London, 1978.

Houser, Preston L., *The Courtyard Gardens of Kyoto*, Suiko Books, Kyoto, 1996.

Inaji, Toshiro, *The Garden As Architecture: Form and Spirit in the Gardens of Japan, China, and Korea*, Kodansha International, Tokyo, 1998.

Itoh, Teiji, *Space and Illusion in the Japanese Garden*, Weatherhill and Tankosha, Tokyo, 1973.

Keane, Marc P., *Japanese Garden Design*, Tuttle Publishing, Tokyo, 1996.

Keane, Marc P., *The Japanese Tea Garden*, Stone Bridge Press, Berkeley, California, 2009.

Koren, Leonard, *Gardens of Gravel and Sand*, Stone Bridge Press, Berkeley, California, 2000.

Kuck, Loraine, *The World of the Japanese Garden: From Chinese Origins to Modern Landscape Art*, Weatherhill, New York, 1984.

Levy, Ian Hideo, *Man'yoshu: A Translation of Japan's Premier Anthology of Classical Poetry*, Vol. 1, Princeton University Press, Princeton, 1981.

Main, Alison, and Platten, Newell, *The Lure of the Japanese Garden*, Wakefield Press, Kent Town, 2002.

Mansfield, Stephen, *Japanese Stone Gardens: Origins, Meaning, Form*, Tuttle Publishing, Tokyo, 2009.

Mehta, K. Geeta, and Tada, Kimie, *Japanese Gardens: Tranquility, Simplicity, Harmony*, Tuttle Publishing, Tokyo, 2008.

Mizuno, Katsuhiko, *Gardens in Kyoto*, Suiko Books, Kyoto, 2002.

Moriguchi, Yasuhiko, and Jenkins, David (trans.), *Hojoki: Visions of a Torn World*, Stone Bridge Press, Berkeley, 1996.

Nitschke, Gunter, *Japanese Gardens: Right Angle and Natural Form*, Taschen, Cologne, 1999.

Nose, Michiko Rico, and Freeman, Michael, *The Modern Japanese Garden*, Octopus, London, 2002.

Rawson, Philip, and Legeza, Laszlo, *Tao: The Eastern Philosophy of Time and Change*, Avon Publishers, New York, 1973.

Shunmyo, Masuno, *Inside Japanese Gardens: From Basics to Planning, Management and Improvement*, The Commemorative Foundation for the International Garden and Greenery Exposition, Osaka, Japan, 1990, Osaka, 2003.

Slawson, David, *Secret Teachings in the Art of Japanese Gardens: Design Principles, Aesthetic Values*, Kodansha, Tokyo, 1987.

Takei, Jiro, and Keane, Marc P., *Sakuteiki: Visions of the Japanese Garden: A Modern Translation of Japan's Gardening Classic*, Tuttle Publishing, Tokyo, 2001.

Treib, Marc and Herman, Ron, *A Guide to the Gardens of Kyoto*, Kodansha International, Tokyo, 2003.

Yamamoto, Kenzo, *Kyoto Gardens*, Suiko Books, Kyoto, 1995.

Young, David and Young, Michiko, *The Art of the Japanese Garden*, Tuttle Publishing, Tokyo, 2005.

Historical Periods

Jomon 10000 BC–300 BC

Yayoi 300 BC–AD 300

Kofun 300–552

Asuka 552–710

Nara 710–794

Heian 94–1185

Kamakura 1185–1333

Muromachi 1333–1568

Momoyama 1568–1600

Edo 1600–1868

Meiji 1868–1912

Taisho 1912–1926

Showa 1926–1989

Heisei 1989–

Glossary

byobu-matsu A form of topiary in which pine trees are shaped into the resemblance of a *byobu* or painted screen.

Daimyo Lords of the provinces. Daimyo gardens were large residential landscapes, often of the stroll garden type.

feng shui Chinese geomancy. Widely applied in adapted form to the design of Japanese gardens and architecture.

fusui Spirit of place. The unique mood and atmospherics associated with scenic nature.

fusuma-e Paintings executed on the surfaces of paper doors.

genkan The entrance area of a house or temple, where shoes are removed and stored.

gohei Ritual paper streamers hung around sacred rocks or beneath the entrance eaves of Shinto shrines.

go-shintai Sacred areas designated in ancient times as dwellings of the gods.

hako-zukuri Box-shaped topiary.

hinbonseki Horizontal stones set in a triad arrangement.

ikedori A term used among Kyoto gardeners to indicate the inclusion of borrowed or captured views in garden design.

iwakura Sacred rocks, usually very large, regarded in pre-Shinto times as seats of the gods.

iwasaka Another term for *iwakura*.

kaiyushiki teien A stroll or circulation garden.

kamejima Turtle islands. The turtle, a felicitous symbol, is associated with longevity.

kami The gods and spirits of the animist and Shinto pantheon.

karesansui A dry landscape garden. Abbreviated to stone garden in common usage.

karikomi The art of topiary.

kohan ni shitagau The gardening custom of "listening" to the request of rocks before deciding where to place them.

meisho Famous sights. In the gardening context, this refers to the reproduction in miniature of scenic spots in Japan and China.

miegakure A hide-and-reveal method used in the stroll garden, whereby scenes are shown and then, as the visitor proceeds along the path, concealed.

mottainai No wastage. The idea of using and recycling objects.

niwa A generic term for garden.

niwa-shi A general term for gardener.

qi The life force contained within all things animate.

roji A tea garden, with the literal meaning of "dewy path."

sanzonseki A rock triad based on the Buddhist trilogy of heaven, man, earth.

sawatobi-ishi Literally, "stepping-stones over a marsh," a path crossing over a section of garden pond.

seki A generic word for stone, rock. *Seki-tei* is another term for stone garden.

shakkei A design method where a landscape or cultural feature outside the garden is co-opted as "borrowed scenery."

shimenawa Sacred straw ropes tied around trees and rocks, marking them as sacred places in Shinto belief.

shisin soo A Chinese concept invoking a quartet of gods that guard the four heavenly directions.

shoin a small study in the residence of an aristocrat, military lord or Zen temple that was expanded into an audience and reception hall. Used for the tea ceremony, it became a *shoin-cha*.

shukkei The miniaturization of famous sights and natural features in the stroll garden.

sukiya A teahouse. The style was adapted for private residences, the term suggesting sophistication in taste.

tsuboniwa A courtyard garden. Sometimes called a *naka-niwa* (inner garden).

tsuridono A fishing pavilion. In the Japanese garden this might be a wooden deck cantilevered over a pond.

tsurujima A garden pond island representing a crane, a symbol like the turtle, of longevity.

yang The Chinese idea of male potency or a positive life force that exists in nature.

yin The negative female counterpart to *yang*.

yohaku no bi The use of empty, but positive, energizing space in gardens and paintings.

yugen An aesthetic of deep, complexly layered beauty.

yuki-tsuri A wigwam-shaped structure made from rice straw that helps to support branches in the event of snowfall.

zazen Seated meditation conducted within a Zen temple.

Zen-tei Literally meaning Zen garden, it is not widely used.

Acknowledgments

Beside nature itself, embattled but still a force to be reckoned with, any author of a book on Japanese gardens is beholden to the great many unknown people who have contributed to their creation. These largely anonymous figures, many of them skillful practitioners at setting stones, managing water flows and applying the principles of geomancy, deserve as much recognition as the patrons and designers of Japanese garden landscapes. Gracious with their time, the ones I have been fortunate enough to meet, were kind enough to answer my many queries, even during the busiest of seasons.

There are always other voices in the background to a book. Among the many garden writers whose works were consulted, and who provided invaluable insights, I would have to include early commentators like Mirei Shigemori, Lorraine Kuck and Ito Teiji, and contemporary authorities such as Gunter Nitschke and David Slawson.

I would like to express my gratitude to the editors and designers who worked on this book for their skillful and creative handling of the material, their intuitive ability to accommodate my preferences. A special thanks is also due to Eric Oey for his vision and enthusiasm in bringing out this, my second garden book with Tuttle.

This book is dedicated to my son Rupert, who, if I am not mistaken, is beginning to develop an appreciation of Japanese gardens.

Left Elegant pavilions are erected to display prize chrysanthemums every autumn at Shinjuku-gyoen.

The Tuttle Story: "Books to Span the East and West"

Most people are surprised when they learn that the world's largest publisher of books on Asia had its beginnings in the tiny American state of Vermont. The company's founder, Charles Tuttle, came from a New England family steeped in publishing, and his first love was books—especially old and rare editions.

Tuttle's father was a noted antiquarian dealer in Rutland, Vermont. Young Charles honed his knowledge of the trade working in the family bookstore, and later in the rare books section of Columbia University Library. His passion for beautiful books—old and new—never wavered through his long career as a bookseller and publisher.

After graduating from Harvard, Tuttle enlisted in the military and in 1945 was sent to Tokyo to work on General Douglas MacArthur's staff. He was tasked with helping to revive the Japanese publishing industry, which had been utterly devastated by the war. After his tour of duty was completed, he left the military, married a talented and beautiful singer, Reiko Chiba, and in 1948 began several successful business ventures.

To his astonishment, Tuttle discovered that postwar Tokyo was actually a book-lover's paradise. He befriended dealers in the Kanda district and began supplying rare Japanese editions to American libraries. He also imported American books to sell to the thousands of GIs stationed in Japan. By 1949, Tuttle's business was thriving, and he opened Tokyo's very first English-language bookstore in the Takashimaya Department Store in Ginza, to great success. Two years later, he began publishing books to fulfill the growing interest of foreigners in all things Asian.

Though a westerner, Charles Tuttle was hugely instrumental in bringing knowledge of Japan and Asia to a world hungry for information about the East. By the time of his death in 1993, he had published over 6,000 books on Asian culture, history and art—a legacy honored by Emperor Hirohito in 1983 with the "Order of the Sacred Treasure," the highest honor Japan bestows upon non-Japanese.

The Tuttle company today maintains an active backlist of some 1,500 titles, many of which have been continuously in print since the 1950s and 1960s—a great testament to Charles Tuttle's skill as a publisher. More than 60 years after its founding, Tuttle Publishing is more active today as at any time in its history, still inspired by Charles' core mission—to publish fine books to span the East and West and provide a greater understanding of each.